GCSE

# Questions and Answers

# Q&A

# CHEMISTRY

KEY STAGE 4


Bob McDuell & Graham Booth

Chief Examiners


SERIES EDITOR: BOB McDUELL

Letts EDUCATIONAL

# Contents


HOW TO USE THIS BOOK 1

THE IMPORTANCE OF USING QUESTIONS FOR REVISION 1

EXAMINATION TECHNIQUE 2

WHICH TIER SHOULD YOU ENTER? 2

TYPES OF EXAMINATION QUESTION 3

ASSESSMENT OBJECTIVES 4

---

QUESTIONS AND REVISION SUMMARIES

1 Structure and bonding 7

2 Oil and carbon chemistry 12

3 Materials from rocks 20

4 Air and atmosphere 30

5 Quantitative chemistry 34

6 The Periodic Table 42

7 Rates of reaction 46

8 Industrial processes 49

9 Water 53

10 Mock examination paper 59

---

ANSWERS 65


---

## HOW TO USE THIS BOOK

The aim of the *Questions and Answers* series is to provide you with help to do as well as possible in your exams at GCSE or, in Scotland, at General and Credit levels. This book is based on the idea that an experienced examiner can give, through examination questions, sample answers and advice, the help students need to secure success and improve their grades.

This *Questions and Answers* series is designed to provide the following.

- **Introductory advice** on the different types of questions and how to answer them to maximise your marks.
- Information about the other skills, apart from the recall of knowledge, that will be tested on examination papers. These are sometimes called **Assessment objectives** and include communication, problem solving, evaluation and interpretation (see pages 4–6). The *Questions and Answers* series is intended to develop these skills by showing you how marks are allocated.
- **Revision summaries** to remind you of the topics you will need to have revised in order to answer examination questions.
- Many examples of **examination questions**, arranged by topic, with spaces for you to fill in your answers, just as on an examination paper. Only try the questions once you have revised a topic thoroughly. Read the Revision summary before attempting the questions to double-check you know the topic. It is best not to consult the answers before trying the questions.
- **Sample answers** to all of the questions.
- **Advice from examiners**. By using the experience of actual Chief Examiners we are able to give advice on how you can improve your answers and avoid the most common mistakes.

## THE IMPORTANCE OF USING QUESTIONS FOR REVISION

Past examination questions play an important part in revising for examinations. However, it is important not to start practising questions too early. Nothing can be more disheartening than trying to do a question which you do not understand because you have not mastered the topic. Therefore, it is important to have studied a topic thoroughly before attempting any questions on it.

How can past examination questions provide a way of preparing for the examination? It is unlikely that any question you try will appear in exactly the same form on the papers you are going to take. However, the examiner is restricted on what can be set because the questions must cover the whole syllabus and test certain Assessment objectives. The number of totally original questions that can be set on any part of the syllabus is very limited and, therefore, similar ideas occur over and over again. Certainly, it will help you if the question you are trying to answer in an examination is familiar and if you know you have done similar questions before. This is a great boost for your confidence and confidence is what is required for examination success.

Practising examination questions will also highlight gaps in your knowledge and understanding, which you can go back to and revise more thoroughly. It will also indicate the sorts of questions you can do well and which, if there is a choice of questions, you should avoid.

Attempting past questions will get you used to the type of language used in questions.

Finally, having access to answers, as you do in this book, will enable you to see clearly what is required by the examiner, how best to answer each question, and the amount of detail required. Attention to detail is a key aspect of achieving success at GCSE.

## EXAMINATION TECHNIQUE

Success in GCSE examinations comes from proper preparation and a positive attitude to the examination. This book is intended to help you overcome 'examination nerves' which often come from a fear of not being properly prepared. Examination technique is extremely important and certainly affects your performance. Remember the basics:

- read the questions carefully;
- make sure that you watch the time carefully and complete the paper – it is no good answering one question well if you spend so long doing it that you do not answer another question at all;
- read the rubric on the front of the examination paper carefully to make sure you know how many questions to attempt;
- examination papers usually tell you how many marks are available for each answer. Take notice of this information as the number of marks gives a guide to the importance of the question and often to the amount you ought to write;
- check before the end of the examination that you have not missed any pages and remember to turn over the last page;
- remember to leave time to check through your work carefully.

## WHICH TIER SHOULD YOU ENTER?

GCSE chemistry papers in England and Wales are set in two tiers – Foundation and Higher. There are only certain grades available for each tier. It is important you enter the correct tier.

| Foundation | Higher |
|---|---|
| | A* |
| | A |
| | B |
| C | C |
| D | D |
| E | |
| F | |
| G | |
| U | |

You can be awarded a C or D grade on either tier. If you are aiming at a grade above C, you need to take the Higher tier. If you are working at D or even C, you are probably better advised to take the Foundation tier, because if you fail to achieve a grade D on Higher tier you will be ungraded.

Approximately 45% of the marks will be on both Higher and Foundation papers. They will be the easy questions on the Higher tier paper and the hard questions on the Foundation tier paper. These questions are used by the examiners to ensure that grades C and D on the two papers are equivalent. If we assume that each paper contains approximately 20% of the marks for each available grade, a Higher tier paper will have a lot of questions which C grade candidates cannot hope to do; the mark required for a grade C on Foundation and Higher will be very different.

## TYPES OF EXAMINATION QUESTION

The questions used on GCSE papers are short answer and structured questions of varying lengths. Most of the questions in this book are of this type. The reason they are used so widely is because they are so versatile. They can be short, with little opportunity for extended writing but giving good syllabus coverage. This makes them very suitable for questions testing lower grades on Foundation tier papers. Alternatively, they can be longer and more complex in their structure, with opportunities for extended writing and the demonstration of higher level of interpretation and evaluation. In this form they are very suitable for questions targeted at A* and A grades on Higher tier papers.

In a structured question, the question is divided into parts (a), (b), (c), etc. These parts can be further subdivided into (i), (ii), (iii), (iv), etc. A structure is built into the question and hence into your answer. This is where the term 'structured question' comes from.

For each part of the question there are a number of lines or a space for your answer. This is a guide to the detail required in the answer, but it does not have to limit you. If you require more space, continue your answer on a separate sheet of paper, but make sure you label the answer clearly, e.g. 3(a)(ii).

For each part of the question there is a number in brackets, e.g. (3), to show you how many marks are allocated to this part of the question by the examiner. If a part is worth three marks, for example, the question requires more than one or two words. As a general rule, if there are three marks allocated, you will need to make three points.

To give you a guide as you work through structured questions, papers are often designed to enable you to score one mark per minute. Therefore, a question worth a maximum of 15 marks should take about 15 minutes to answer.

You do not have to write your answers in full sentences. Concise notes are often the most suitable response.

As with all questions, it is most important to read the stimulus material in the question thoroughly and more than once. This information is often not used fully by students and, as a result, the question is not answered fully. The key to answering many of these questions comes from the appreciation of the full meaning of the 'command word' at the start of the question – for example 'state', 'describe' or 'explain'. The following glossary of command words may help you in the answering of structured questions.

- **State** This means a brief answer is required, with no supporting evidence. Alternatives include **write down**, **give**, **list** and **name**.
- **Define** Just a definition is required.
- **State and explain** A short answer is required (see **state**) but then an explanation is required. A question of this type should be worth more than one mark.
- **Describe** This is often used with reference to a particular experiment. The important points should be given about each stage. Again, this type of question is worth more than one mark.
- **Outline** The answer should be brief and the main points picked out.
- **Predict** A brief answer is required, without supporting evidence. You are required to make logical links between various pieces of information.
- **Complete** You are required to add information to a diagram, sentence, flow chart, graph, key, table, etc.
- **Find** This is a general term, which may mean calculate, measure, determine, etc.
- **Calculate** A numerical answer is required. You should show your working in order to get an answer. Do not forget the correct units.
- **Suggest** There is not just one correct answer, or you are applying your answer to a situation outside the syllabus.

## Grid questions

These are another type of multiple-choice question used on chemistry papers by the Scottish Examination Board.

In these questions you have to circle the appropriate letter or letters in the answer grid, e.g.

| | | |
|---|---|---|
| A $CH_4$ | B $H_2$ | C $CO_2$ |
| D $CO$ | E $C_2H_5OH$ | F $C$ |

(a) Identify the hydrocarbon(s).

[*The question does not tell you whether one or more than one substance is required. The only correct answer is **A** and you should circle this letter in the grid. A hydrocarbon is a compound of hydrogen and carbon only. If you circle too many answers, you lose marks.*]

(b) Identify the substance(s) which can burn to produce **both** carbon dioxide and water.

[*Again the question does not tell you how many answers to give. The correct answers are **A** and **E** – the only ones where carbon and hydrogen are combined together.*]

# ASSESSMENT OBJECTIVES

Assessment objectives are the intellectual and practical skills you should be able to show. Opportunities must be made by the examiner when setting the examination paper for you to demonstrate your mastery of these skills when you answer the question paper.

Traditionally, the Assessment objective of knowledge and understanding has been regarded as the most important skill to develop. Candidates have been directed to learn large bodies of knowledge to recall in the examination. Whilst not wanting in any way to devalue the learning of facts, it should be remembered that on modern papers knowledge and understanding can only contribute about half of the marks available. The other half of the marks are acquired by mastery of the other Assessment objectives. These are to:

- communicate scientific observations, ideas and arguments effectively;
- select and use reference materials and to translate data from one form to another;
- interpret, evaluate and make informed judgements from relevant facts, observations and phenomena;
- solve qualitative and quantitative problems.

## 1 Communicate scientific observations, ideas and arguments effectively

(*weighting on papers approximately 5–10%*)

In any examination, communication of information to the examiner is of primary importance. Questions are built into the paper to test your ability to communicate scientific information. Often these questions require extended answers.

In this type of question it is important to look at your answer objectively after you have written it to try to judge whether your answer is communicating information effectively.

## 2 Select and use reference materials and translate data from one form to another (*weighting on papers approximately 10–15%*)

In questions testing this Assessment objective you are frequently asked to pick information from a chart or table and use it in another form, e.g. to draw a graph, a pie chart, bar chart, etc. You may be asked to complete a table using information from a graph.

It is important to transfer the skills you have acquired in mathematics to your work in chemistry.

| Skill acquired | Approx. grade in GCSE maths |
|---|---|
| Read information from graphs or simple diagrams | F |
| Work out simple percentages | F |
| Construct and use pie charts | F |
| Use graphs | E |
| Plot graphs from data provided (the axes and scales are given to you) | E |
| Be able to draw the best line through points on a graph | C |
| Select the most appropriate axes and scales for graph plotting | B |

It is reasonable, therefore, to conclude that at Higher tier you might be required to use a blank piece of graph paper and choose your own scales and axes. Then you would plot the points and draw a line of best fit through the points. If you are doing this, remember the following.

❶ To draw your graph as large as possible on the graph paper by choosing scales appropriately. Avoid choosing scales where, for example, three small squares are equivalent to 5°C. It would be better if one small square were equivalent to 1°C or 2°C. With this type of graph drawing, marks are usually awarded for the choice of scales and for labelled axes.

❷ To plot each point with a dot or small cross. Circle the dot or cross to make its position clear.

❸ Your line of best fit, whether it is a straight line or a curve, does not have to go through all the points. Some points may not be in the correct place, even if you plotted them correctly, because of inaccuracies in the experiment or experimental error.

On a Foundation tier paper a similar graph may have to be drawn, but it would be more appropriate for the examiner to give a grid with axes and scales given. Then you would only have to plot the points and draw the line of best fit.

### 3 Interpret, evaluate and make informed judgements from relevant facts, observations and phenomena *(weighting on papers approximately 10–15%)*

Questions testing this Assessment objective are often difficult for candidates. It is much easier to test this on a Higher tier paper than on a Foundation tier paper.

The command word 'suggest' is very frequently used, as the information given, perhaps in a paragraph, a table or diagram (or any combination of these), is open to more than one interpretation.

Look carefully at all of the information given and look for possible alternative interpretations before writing your answer.

### 4 Solve qualitative and quantitative problems *(weighting on papers approximately 10–15%)*

There is no shortage of opportunities to ask questions testing this Assessment objective on GCSE chemistry papers. Again opportunities are greater, especially for solving quantitative problems, on Higher tier papers.

Qualitative problems can include writing equations and the use of qualitative tests, for example, to distinguish sulphuric and hydrochloric acids.

Quantitative problems include the full range of chemical calculations – which, for generations, have baffled students studying chemistry. Remember, when attempting to carry out a chemical calculation, to:

❶ use all of the information given to you (if the question gives relative atomic masses, they should be used);

❷ show all of your working, so credit can be given if you do not get the correct answer but get some way through the question;

❸ take care when substituting in a mathematical formula to be consistent in your units;

❹ give correct units to your answers if there are units (remember ratios, including relative atomic masses, do not have units).

Throughout this book you will see questions which are designed to test Assessment objectives other than knowledge and understanding.

# Structure and bonding 1

**REVISION SUMMARY**

There are three states of matter – **solid**, **liquid** and **gas**. All matter can exist in any of these states, depending upon conditions of temperature and pressure. In all three states the material is made up of particles

In a solid the particles are vibrating about fixed positions. If the solid is crystalline, the particles are regularly arranged and usually closely packed. In a liquid the particles are still close together, but there is no regular arrangement. There is more movement of particles and the movement increases as temperature rises. In the gas state the particles have broken away from each other and are free to move around.

When a change of state occurs, e.g. solid to liquid, there is an associated energy change. In this case, energy is required to break up the solid structure and give the particles additional kinetic energy. The reverse process – liquid to solid – will release energy. **Diffusion** is the movement of particles to spread out and fill all of the available space. Diffusion takes place rapidly with gases, because the particles in a gas are moving rapidly. It takes place more slowly in liquids and solids, because there is less movement of particles.

Elements are composed of atoms. A piece of iron is made up solely of iron atoms. In a mixture, there will be different types of atom, and the atoms of the different elements will not be joined. In a compound, again there will be atoms of different elements, but they will be joined together. A mixture of hydrogen and oxygen can consist of hydrogen and oxygen in different proportions, but water (a compound of hydrogen and oxygen) always contains twice as many atoms of hydrogen as oxygen. Groups of atoms in elements or compounds are called **molecules**. An oxygen molecule consists of a pair of oxygen atoms together ($O_2$) and a water molecule consists of two hydrogen atoms and one oxygen ($H_2O$).

Atoms of the different elements are made up of different numbers of protons, neutrons and electrons. An atom always contains an equal number of protons and electrons. If an atom loses one or more electrons, it forms a **positive ion** or **cation**. If an atom gains one or more electrons, it forms a **negative ion** or **anion**. Atoms of the same element must contain the same number of protons and electrons, but can contain different numbers of neutrons. These are called **isotopes**. The protons and neutrons make up the positively charged nucleus and the electrons move around the nucleus.

There are two methods commonly used to join or **bond** atoms together. **Ionic bonding**, e.g. sodium chloride, involves the complete transfer of one or more electron from a metal atom to a non-metal atom. This forms ions, which are held together by strong electrostatic forces. **Covalent bonding**, e.g. chlorine or hydrogen chloride, involves the sharing of pairs of electrons.

The properties of a material are related to the structure of the material. If the material is made up of molecules, it will have a low melting and boiling point. If it is made up of a **giant structure** of atoms or ions, it will have a high melting point. A giant structure of ions produces a melt which conducts electricity.

Chemical reactions which release energy are called **exothermic** reactions and ones which take in energy are called **endothermic** reactions. These can be represented in energy level diagrams.

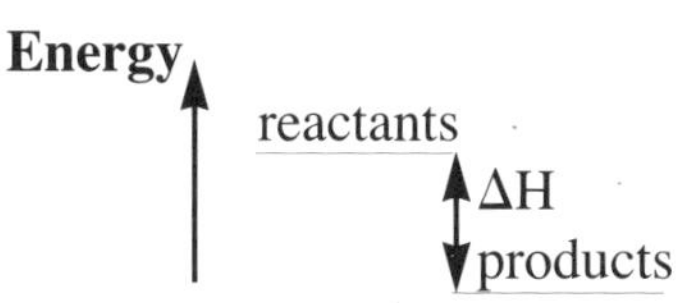


**exothermic**

**endothermic**

When chemical bonds are broken, energy is used, and energy is produced when bonds are formed. If a reaction is exothermic (gives out energy) the energy produced by the bonds formed is greater than the energy required to break the bonds.

**If you need to revise this subject more thoroughly, see the relevant topics in the Letts GCSE *Chemistry Study Guide*, or *CD-ROM*.**

QUESTIONS

1 The diagrams show the outer electron arrangements in atoms of hydrogen and chlorine.

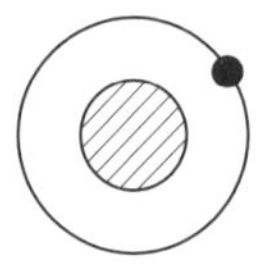
hydrogen atom

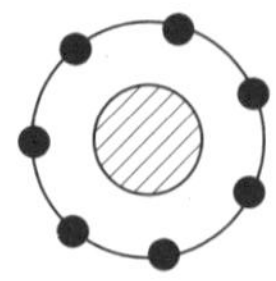
chlorine atom
(not to scale)

(a) Draw diagrams to show the arrangement of the outer electrons in

(i) a hydrogen molecule, $H_2$

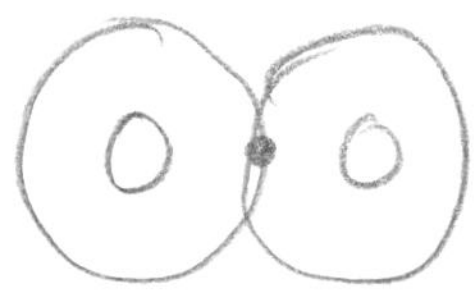

(ii) a chlorine molecule, $Cl_2$

(2)

(b) What type of bonding is present in both a hydrogen molecule and a chlorine molecule?

covalent bonds (1)

(c) Explain why the boiling point of chlorine is greater than the boiling point of fluorine, $F_2$, but less than the boiling point of bromine, $Br_2$.

chlorine has a much Stronger bond and
So Some thing like flarine with a poor bond
will break up easly. Bromine has a strong bond and so high BP. (3)

(d) Dry hydrogen chloride, HCl, is a gas. It dissolves in water, producing heat energy and a solution which conducts electricity.
Describe the changes in bonding when dry hydrogen chloride is dissolved in water.

..............................

..............................

.............................. (3)

Letts Q&A

QUESTIONS

**2** There are two different types of lithium atom, ${}^{6}_{3}Li$ and ${}^{7}_{3}Li$. Lithium has a relative atomic mass of 6.9.

(a) What name is used to describe the different types of lithium atom?

Isotope (1)

(b) What can be said about the proportions of each type of atom in lithium?

${}^{7}_{3}Li$ has one more electron than ${}^{6}_{3}Li$

but they both have the same number of protons

(1)

(c) Complete the table to show the numbers of protons, neutrons and electrons in the ${}^{7}_{3}Li^{+}$ ion.

| **Particle** | **Number** |
|---|---|
| protons | 3 |
| neutrons | 3 |
| electrons | 4 |

(2)

*SQA 1995*

**3** The diagram shows a simple representation of the particles in a gas.

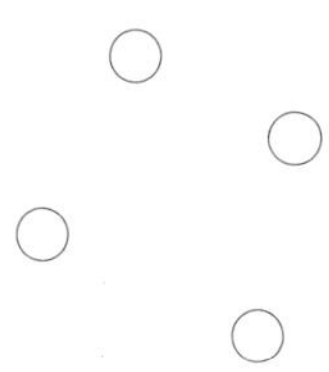

(a) Describe the movement of the particles in a gas.

very free flowing as apposed to a liquid (1)

(b) Why does increasing the temperature of the gas increase the pressure of the gas?

Because they become more active in order to hit

all the sides more and generally expand. (2)

Letts Q&A

QUESTIONS

(c) Sulphur dioxide gas and hydrogen sulphide gas react. The symbolic equation is

$$2H_2S(g) + SO_2(g) \rightarrow 3S(s) + 2H_2O(l)$$

A long tube was clamped horizontally. A pad of cotton wool soaked in hydrogen sulphide solution (giving off hydrogen sulphide gas) and a pad soaked in sulphur dioxide solution (giving off sulphur dioxide gas) were placed at the same time in opposite ends of the tube.

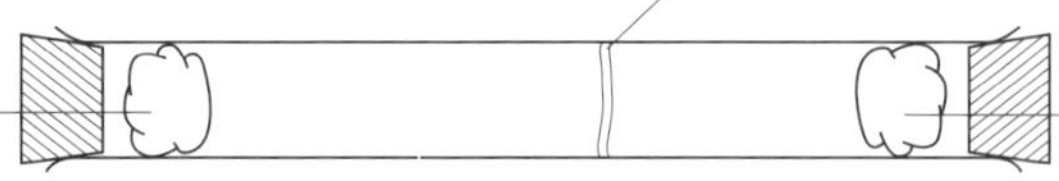


After five minutes a band of whitish solid was formed inside the tube.

(i) What is the whitish solid formed in the tube?

Sulpher .......... (1)

(ii) The solid formed because of the movement of hydrogen sulphide and sulphur dioxide particles. What is this movement of particles called?

Deffusion .......... (1)

(iii) What does the experiment tell you about the movement of hydrogen sulphide and sulphur dioxide particles?

hydrogen Sulphide moves faster .......... (1)

(iv) Why does it take so long for the band of solid to form?

Because it is in the air and not

in a Solution .......... (2)

Letts Q&A

**4** The table gives some of the properties of six substances A–F.

| Substance | Density (g per cm$^3$) | Melting point (°C) | Boiling point (°C) | Electrical conductivity | Other properties |
|---|---|---|---|---|---|
| A | 0.97 | 98 | 883 | conductor | forms a basic oxide |
| B | 3.51 | > 3550 | 4827 | non-conductor | forms an acidic oxide |
| C | 2.25 | 3680 | 4827 | conductor | forms an acidic oxide |
| D | 3.12 | −7 | 59 | non-conductor | does not burn |
| E | 0.001 | −169 | −104 | non-conductor | burns to form $CO_2$ and $H_2O$ only |
| F | 2.17 | 801 | 1413 | non-conductor when solid; conductor when molten | dissolves in water |

(a) Using the information in the table, write down the letter of the substance that:

(i) is a liquid at room temperature and pressure ......D......

(ii) has the most widely spaced particles ......E......

(iii) is a metal ......C......

(iv) is a solid which floats on water ......A......

(v) has a giant ionic structure ......A......

(vi) has a giant atomic (macromolecular) structure ......B...... (6)

(You can use a letter once, more than once or not at all.)

(b) B and C are different forms of the same element in the same state.

(i) What name is given to the different forms of the same element in the same state?

......Allotrobe...... (1)

(ii) What evidence is there in the table that B and C are the same element?

......Same Boiling point and Similar melting point and forms acid...... (1)

(iii) What evidence is there that B and C are non-metallic?

......B is none conductive and so C cannot be matalic...... (1)

# 2 Oil and carbon chemistry

## REVISION SUMMARY

The study of the chemistry of carbon compounds, excluding some simple compounds such as carbon dioxide and carbon monoxide, is called **organic chemistry**. There is a very large number of carbon compounds because of the stable bonds formed by carbon atoms with other carbon atoms and with atoms of a range of other elements.

Petroleum (crude oil) is a source of hydrocarbons widely used in the chemical industry. Fractional distillation separates petroleum into different fractions, each containing a number of chemical compounds which boil within a range of temperature.

Most of the compounds making up petroleum are **alkanes**. These are a homologous series of **hydrocarbons** (compounds of carbon and hydrogen only) which all fit a general formula of $C_nH_{2n+2}$. The simplest members are:

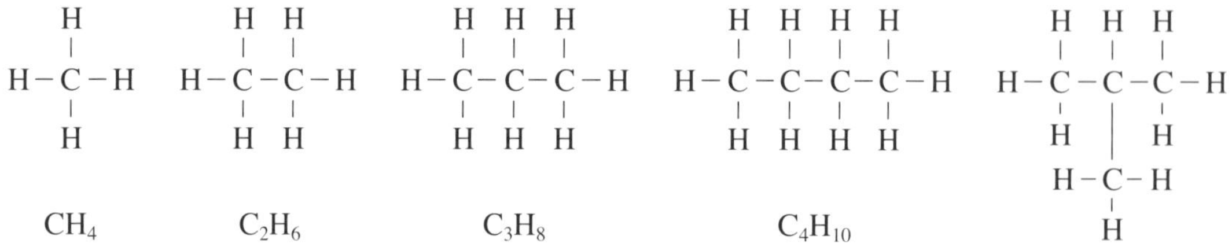

$CH_4$ methane, $C_2H_6$ ethane, $C_3H_8$ propane, $C_4H_{10}$ n-butane, isobutane

There are two **isomers** of butane because alternative arrangements of the atoms are possible. All alkanes are **saturated**, i.e. they contain only carbon–carbon single bonds. Alkanes make good fuels, but are otherwise unreactive.

**Cracking** is used to break long-chain alkanes into smaller molecules. The products of cracking depend upon conditions. Some of the molecules produced are **unsaturated** and belong to the homologous series of **alkenes**. Alkenes fit a general formula $C_nH_{2n}$ and contain a carbon–carbon double bond. The simplest alkene is ethene, $C_2H_4$. The presence of a carbon–carbon double bond (or triple bond) can be detected by using bromine dissolved in a suitable solvent (e.g. hexane). The bromine solution turns from red-brown to colourless.

Alkenes are much more reactive than alkanes. Like alkanes they burn, but they also take part in addition reactions, e.g.

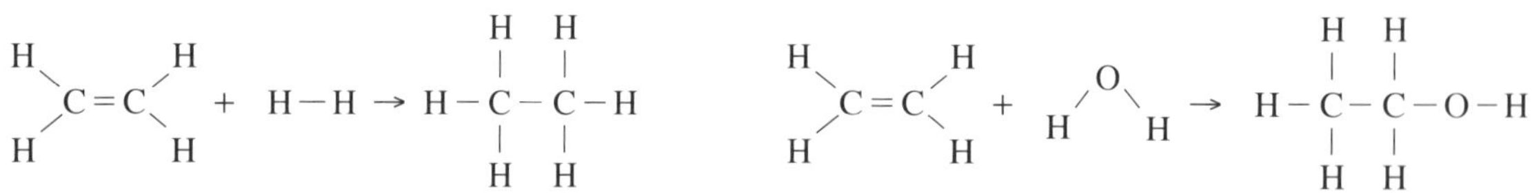

ethene + hydrogen → ethane ethene + water → ethanol

Manufacturing margarine is an important industrial process which uses the addition of hydrogen to unsaturated molecules. Animal and vegetable oils, the raw material, contain carbon–carbon double bonds and are liquid. The corresponding saturated compounds are suitable for use as margarine as they are solid. Hydrogen gas is passed through the oil in the presence of a nickel catalyst at 140° C. Hydrogenation (reaction with hydrogen takes place).

Ethanol (sometimes called alcohol) can be produced from ethene by an addition reaction. It can also be produced by **fermentation**. Fermentation is the action of enzymes on a solution of sugar or starch.

$$\underset{\text{glucose}}{C_6H_{12}O_6} \rightarrow \underset{\text{ethanol}}{2C_2H_5OH} + \underset{\text{carbon dioxide}}{2CO_2}$$

The solution produced by fermentation is a dilute solution of ethanol in water. The ethanol can be made more concentrated by fractional distillation.

**REVISION SUMMARY**

Many of the items which used to be made from metals are now made of plastic materials called **polymers**. There are many polymers which exist in nature, e.g. cellulose, starch and proteins. They are called **natural polymers**. Probably more important to us today for manufacturing items are factory-made **synthetic polymers**. Examples are poly(ethene), polystyrene and nylon. There are two types of polymerisation – **addition polymerisation** and **condensation polymerisation**.

In addition polymerisation the monomers contain a carbon–carbon double bond. The molecules join together without losing any atoms.

$$n\text{M} \rightarrow (\text{M})_n$$

An example of addition polymerisation is making poly(ethene).

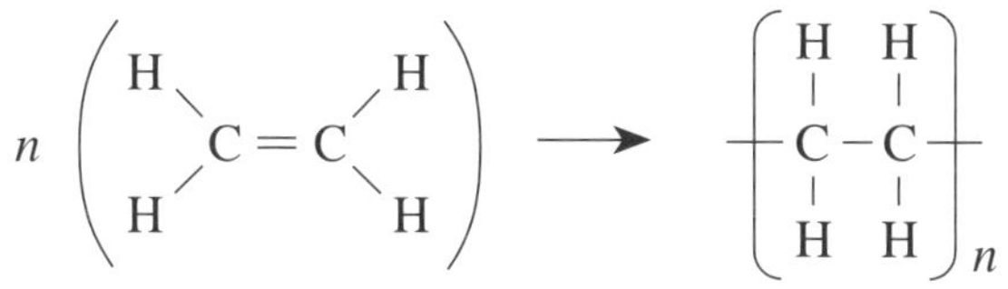

The polymer does not contain the double bond present in the monomer.

When condensation polymerisation takes place, the monomer molecules lose small molecules, such as water or hydrogen chloride, when they join together. The monomer molecules must contain two reactive groups. Nylon-6,6 is made from polymerising hexane-1,6-diamine and hexanedioic acid. The process is summarised as:

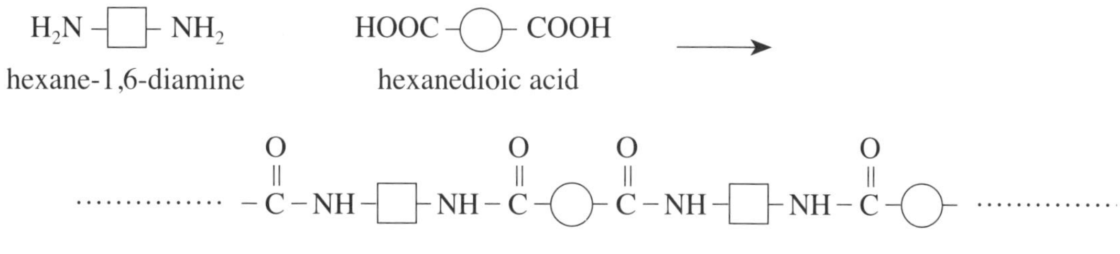


Polymers can be divided into two classes, depending on how they change on heating. **Thermoplastics** soften on heating and then turn solid again on cooling. Therefore, they are easily moulded. **Thermosetting** polymers do not melt on heating, but at a higher temperature may burn or decompose.

Starch is a natural polymer made in green plants by photosynthesis. Starch is a carbohydrate (a compound of carbon, hydrogen and oxygen fitting a formula $C_xH_{2y}O_y$), made by linking together glucose molecules. Glucose is the monomer and a water molecule is eliminated each time a link is made. Starch is broken down in the digestive system by hydrolysis. The enzyme in saliva (amylase) breaks down the starch to produce a sugar called maltose (two glucose units joined together). Hydrolysis with acid produces glucose.

Proteins are made by joining together monomer molecules called amino acids. There are about 20 amino acids which join together to form proteins. The links between amino acids are called peptide links.

**If you need to revise this subject more thoroughly, see the relevant topics in the *Letts GCSE Chemistry Study Guide*, or *CD-ROM*.**

**QUESTIONS**

1 An organic compound, X, contains only the three elements carbon, hydrogen and oxygen. It contains 37.5% carbon and 12.5% hydrogen.
($A_r$(C) = 12, $A_r$(H) = 1, $A_r$(O) = 16)

(a) Use the information to find the empirical formula of X.

Persentage of oxygen = 50%

37.5/12 moles, 12.5/1 moles, 50/16 moles

3.125 moles C, 12.5 moles of H 3.125 moles of O

1 C 4 H 1 O CH4O (4)

X can be oxidised, under suitable conditions, to form an acid, Y.

(b) Suggest a structural formula for X.

(1)

(c) What homologous series does X belong to?

.................................................................... (1)

(d) Suggest an identity for the acid Y.

.................................................................... (1)

2 (a) Crude oil consists of a large number of different compounds. Most of these compounds are *alkanes*.

(i) Explain how fractional distillation separates crude oil.

At different temperatures different compounds evaporate

So heating In stages Separates them out

.................................................................... (2)

(ii) What are *alkanes*?

It is a Soap the opposit of a acid

and the higher end of the Ph balence 7–14 (2)

(iii) Alkanes, such as methane, $CH_4$, are used as fuels. Write a balanced chemical equation for the complete combustion of methane in oxygen.

CH4 + O2 → CHO2 .................................................... (3)

(b) Alkenes can be made by cracking large alkane molecules.

(i) Explain how the cracking process is carried out.

....................................................................................................

....................................................................................................

....................................................................................................

.................................................................................................... (2)

(ii) Give a chemical test which would show the difference between an alkene and an alkane.

Test Bromin ....................................................................................

Result of test Saturated - No colour change ....................................

unsaturated - goes translucent .................................................. (2)

(c) Alkenes, such as ethene, can be made into polymers.

(i) Complete the following to show how the ethene molecules bond to form part of a polymer.

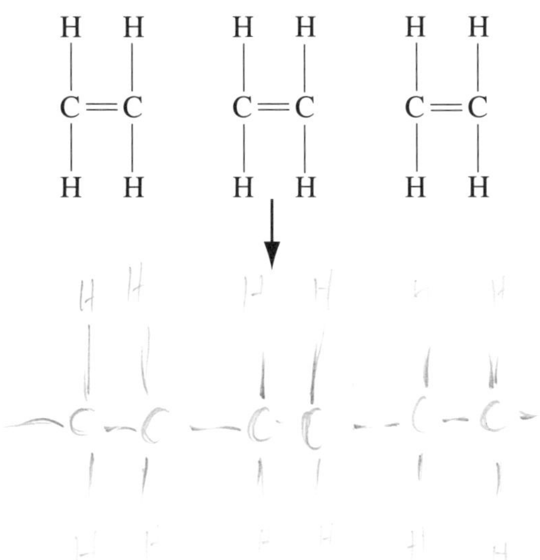

(1)

(ii) Name the polymer formed from ethene.

Polyethene ................................................................................................ (1)

(iii) Explain **one** important problem caused by the everyday use of this polymer.

Polution when it is made ................................................................................................

................................................................................................

................................................................................................ (2)

*SEG 1998*

**3** The flow chart outlines some useful products which can be obtained from crude oil. Crude oil is a mixture of hydrocarbons.

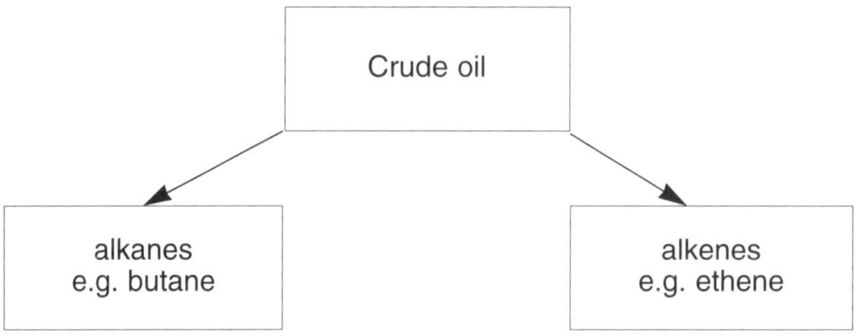


(a) (i) The molecular formula of butane is $C_4H_{10}$. Draw a structural formula for butane.

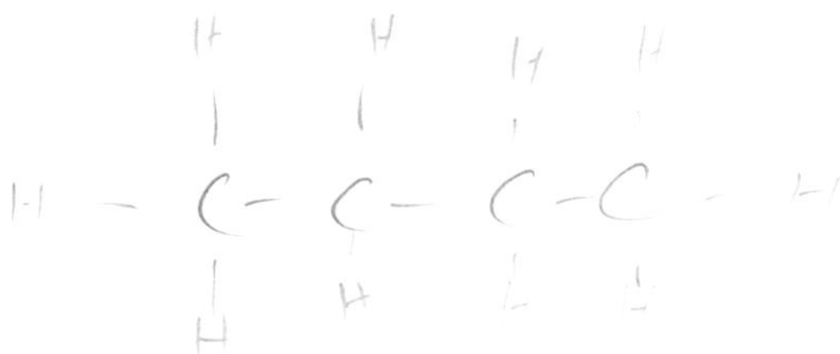

(1)

(ii) The molecular formula for ethene is $C_2H_4$. Draw a structural formula for ethene.

(1)

(b) Ethene and butane react with bromine:

$$C_2H_4 + Br_2 \rightarrow C_2H_4Br_2$$

$$C_4H_{10} + Br_2 \rightarrow C_4H_9Br + HBr$$

(i) State the conditions needed for each reaction.

Reaction with ethene ...... Heat ......

..............................................................................

Reaction with butane ...... Heat + pressure ......

.............................................................................. (2)

(ii) Name the type of reaction when bromine reacts with:

Ethene ..............................................................................

Butane .............................................................................. (2)

(iii) Draw the full structural formula of each organic product, showing all bonds.

Product from reaction with ethene:

Product from reaction with butane:

(2)

QUESTIONS

(c) (i) Write a balanced chemical equation for the combustion of butane in oxygen.

$2C_4H_{10} + 13O_2 \rightarrow 4CO_2\ 10H_2O$ ........................ (2)

(ii) Use your equation to calculate the volume of oxygen needed to burn 1 $dm^3$ of butane at room conditions. (1 mole of gas occupies 24 $dm^3$ at room conditions.)

6½

2 13

Answer 1 mole of Butane to 6½ of Oxygen ........................ (2)

*SEG 1996*

**4** (a) (i) Name the series of hydrocarbons with the general formula $C_nH_{2n+2}$.

........................................................................................................ (1)

(ii) Give the combustion products of hydrocarbons when they undergo:

I. Complete combustion

.......................................................... and ..........................................................

II. Incomplete combustion

.......................................................... and .......................................................... (4)

(b) Another series of hydrocarbons has the general formula $C_nH_{2n}$.
Ethene is the first member of this series.

(i) Complete the following diagram by putting the reaction conditions or formula of the products in the appropriate box.

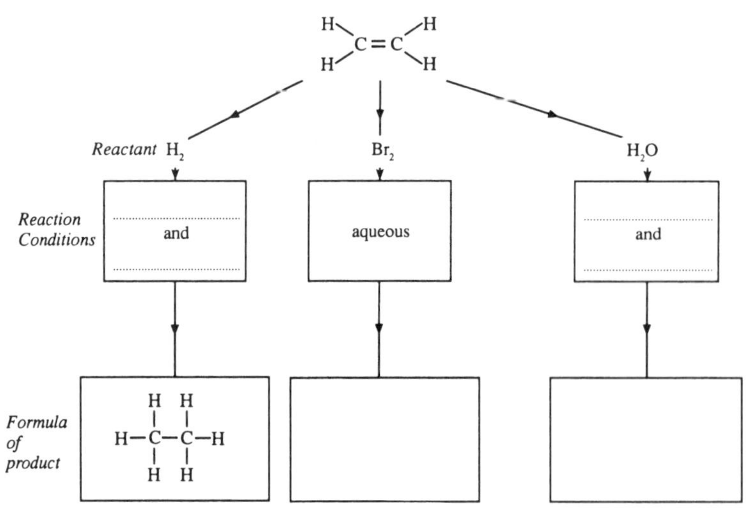


(4)

QUESTIONS

(ii) Which **one** of these three reactions is similar to that used for manufacturing margarine?

.................................................................................................................... (1)

(iii) What is the starting material used for manufacturing margarine?

.................................................................................................................... (1)

(c) (i) Draw the structure of **methanol**, $CH_3OH$.

(1)

(ii) For the formation of ethanol from sugar, state the other **reactant(s)** required and the **conditions** necessary for a reaction. Name also the **main by-product**.

Reactant(s) ..........................................................................................

Conditions ..........................................................................................

Main by-product ................................................................................ (4)

(iii) In addition to alcoholic drinks give **two** other uses of ethanol.

....................................................................................................................

and

.................................................................................................................... (2)

*WJEC 1997*

# 3 Materials from rocks

## REVISION SUMMARY

There are three parts which make up the Earth – the **crust**, the **mantle** and the **core**. The crust is a thin layer of surface rocks, between 7 km and 40 km thick. Underneath the crust is the mantle and in the centre of the Earth is the core. Our understanding of the structure of the core comes from studies including the passage of sound waves through the Earth. These studies, called seismic studies, show scientists that the inner core of the Earth is solid.

The work of Alfred Wegener showed that the Earth's crust is made up from a number of huge **plates** which are floating on the liquid magma. Originally the plates made up one supercontinent called Pangaea. These plates are moving very slowly – perhaps only a few centimetres a year. The movement of these plates is called **plate tectonics**.

Where two plates are sliding past each other, they produce stresses and strains which may be released suddenly in an **earthquake**. When two plates are moving apart, a crack will appear in the Earth's crust. Molten rock from the mantle will come to the surface and new rocks will be formed. This often takes place under oceans and is not easily seen. This is called a **constructive plate margin**.

When two plates collide, rocks are squeezed together. This causes the pushing of one plate upwards to create a mountain range. The Himalayas were formed from the collision of the Eurasian and Indian plates. Alternatively, one of the plates is pushed back downwards into the magma. This is called a **destructive plate margin**.

The rocks of the Earth can be classified as igneous, metamorphic and sedimentary.

- **Igneous rocks** are formed when molten magma from inside the Earth is cooled. They are crystalline and the size of the crystals depends upon the rate of cooling. Large crystals are formed when the cooling is slow. There are two types of igneous rocks – **intrusive** rocks (e.g. granite), which are formed inside the Earth, and **extrusive** rocks (e.g. basalt), which are formed on the surface of the Earth.
- **Metamorphic rocks** are formed when high temperatures and pressures act on sedimentary and igneous rocks. Marble is a metamorphic rock produced from limestone.
- **Sedimentary rocks** are formed when rocks in the Earth are eroded and the sediments are transported and deposited. When these layers of rock fragments are compressed over a long period, sedimentary rocks are formed. Chalk is a sedimentary rock.

Rocks are being continuously recycled in the rock cycle.

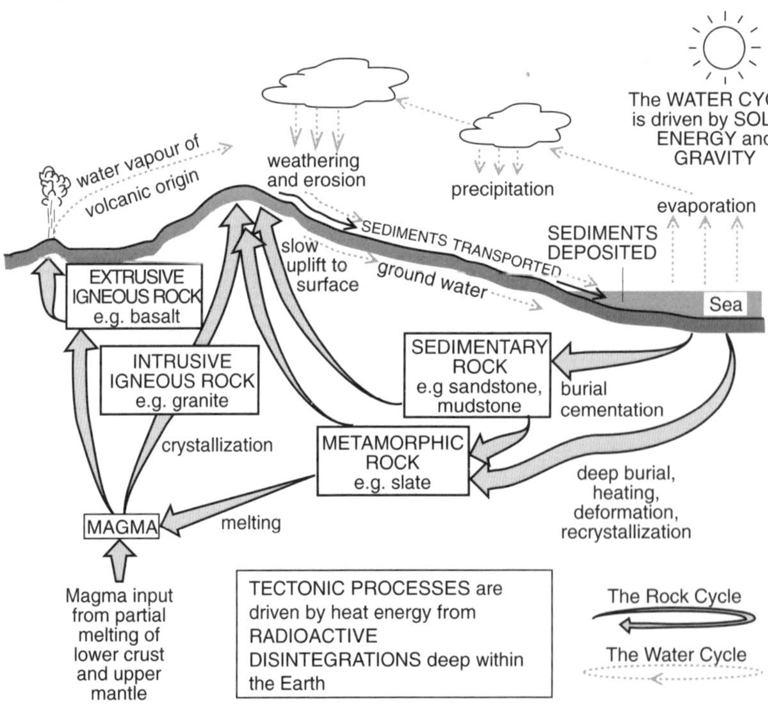

REVISION SUMMARY

Rocks are used for a wide range of purposes – for building materials and as a source of raw material for making useful products. Metals are extracted from metal ores. The method of extraction is related to the reactivity of the metal.

Most metals react with oxygen, water and acids, but at different rates. Metals are often arranged in order of reactivity, called a **reactivity series**.

Such a series is:

K Na Ca Mg Al Zn Fe Pb Cu Ag

→ decreasing reactivity

A reactivity series can be used to predict the products of a chemical reaction.

e.g. copper(II) sulphate + iron → copper + iron(II) sulphate

A reaction takes place because iron is more reactive than copper (higher in the reactivity series).

Metals high in the reactivity series are extracted from their ores by electrolysis. **Electrolysis** involves the **decomposition** of an **electrolyte** using electricity. Electrolysis takes place when ions are free to move when an electrolyte is molten or dissolved in water. The products of electrolysis are formed at the electrodes.

e.g. lead(II) bromide (molten) → lead (formed at the negative electrode called the cathode) + bromine (formed at the positive electrode called the anode)

Metals and hydrogen are usually produced at the cathode and oxygen or one of the halogens at the anode. Ionic equations are often used to represent changes taking place at the electrodes.

Cathode: $Pb^{2+} + 2e^- \rightarrow Pb$ Anode: $2Br^- \rightarrow Br_2 + 2e^-$

Metals in the middle of the reactivity series are usually extracted by reduction of the ore with carbon. Metals low in the reactivity series are often found uncombined in the Earth or are extracted simply by heating.

Questions on the extraction of the metals aluminium and iron are frequently asked on GCSE chemistry papers.

## Extraction of aluminium

Bauxite is the ore of aluminium. It contains hydrated aluminium oxide $Al_2O_33H_2O$. The ore is purified to produce alumina-pure aluminium oxide, $Al_2O_3$. Aluminium is high in the reactivity series and aluminium oxide is difficult to split up. Electrolysis has to be used.

Aluminium is obtained by the electrolysis of alumina dissolved in molten cryolite (sodium aluminium fluoride, $Na_3AlF_6$). The anode and cathode are made of carbon.

The electrode reactions taking place are:

Cathode $Al^{3+} + 3e^- \rightarrow Al$

Anode $2O^{2-} \rightarrow O_2 + 4e^-$

The carbon anode burns in the oxygen produced and has to be regularly replaced. Aluminium is tapped off from the cells.

The process takes a great deal of electricity. To produce 1 tonne of aluminium requires 17 000 kW of electricity, enough electricity for the consumption of a fairly large town for 1 hour.

Letts Q&A

REVISION SUMMARY

## Extraction of iron

Iron is extracted in a continuous process in a blast furnace. The blast furnace is loaded with iron ore (haematite, $Fe_2O_3$), coke and limestone. The furnace is heated with blasts of hot air. The reactions taking place are:

1. $C + O_2 \rightarrow CO_2$
2. $CO_2 + C \rightarrow 2CO$
3. $Fe_2O_3 + 3CO \rightarrow 2Fe + 3CO_2$
4. $CaCO_3 \rightarrow CaO + CO_2$
5. $CaO + SiO_2 \rightarrow CaSiO_3$

In the important step 3 iron(III) oxide is reduced to iron by carbon monoxide. Impurities such as silicon dioxide are removed from the furnace in step 5, where basic and acidic oxides react to form calcium silicate (called slag).

Molten impure iron (called pig iron) and molten slag are tapped off at the bottom of the furnace.

Most of the pig iron produced is turned into steel. In the steel-making process, oxygen gas is blown through molten iron to convert impurities such as carbon, sulphur and phosphorus into acidic oxides which escape as gases or react with added calcium oxide. Scrap iron can be added to the steel-making furnace to reduce the amount of pig iron required. Finally, carbon can be added to produce steel with the required specification.

Steel is an **alloy** of iron, i.e. a mixture of iron with small quantities of carbon and possibly other metals. The addition of small quantities of other metals or carbon alters the properties of iron. High carbon steel is strong but brittle. Low carbon steel is soft and is easily shaped. Stainless steel, which contains chromium and nickel, is hard and resistant to corrosion.

**If you need to revise this subject more thoroughly, see the relevant topics in the Letts GCSE *Chemistry Study Guide*, or *CD-ROM*.**

QUESTIONS

1 The Earth's surface is the top of a solid crust which is made up of plates. These plates move slowly. The crust under the continents is about 35 km thick and has an average density of about 2.7 $g/cm^3$. The crust under the ocean floor is much thinner and has an average density of about 3.3 $g/cm^3$. The material underneath the crust has an average density of about 4.5 $g/cm^3$.
The average density of the Earth is 5.5 $g/cm^3$.

(a) What evidence is there to suggest that there is a dense metal core at the centre of the Earth?

..........................................................................................................................................

.......................................................................................................................................... (1)

(b) Continental plates often collide with ocean floor plates. Describe what is likely to happen when a continental plate meets an ocean plate moving in the opposite direction. Explain your answer. A diagram may help you with your answer.

(3)

(c) Explain how earthquakes can occur where two plates meet together.

..........................................................................................................................................

.......................................................................................................................................... (2)

(d) What evidence suggests that there may be molten material underneath the Earth's crust?

.......................................................................................................................................... (1)

QUESTIONS

(e) The map shows the 'supercontinent' called Pangaea.

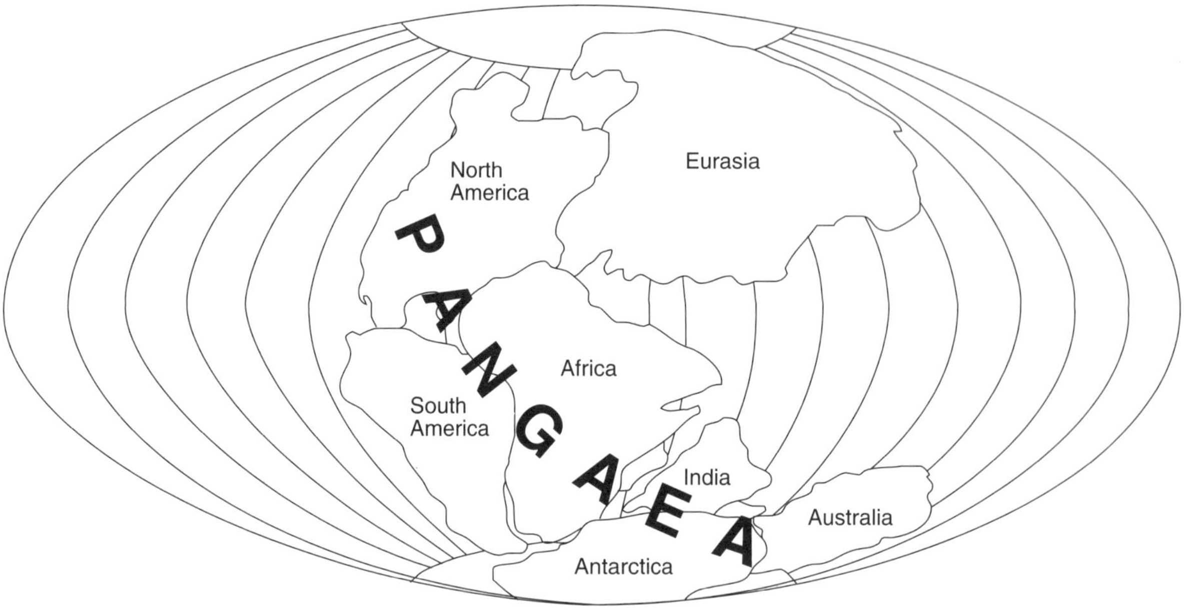


How does the theory of plate tectonics explain the existence of similar fossils and rocks in South America and Africa?

.......................................................................................................................

....................................................................................................................... (2)

**2** This question is about rocks in the Earth and the way they are recycled. The following diagram may help you with your answers.

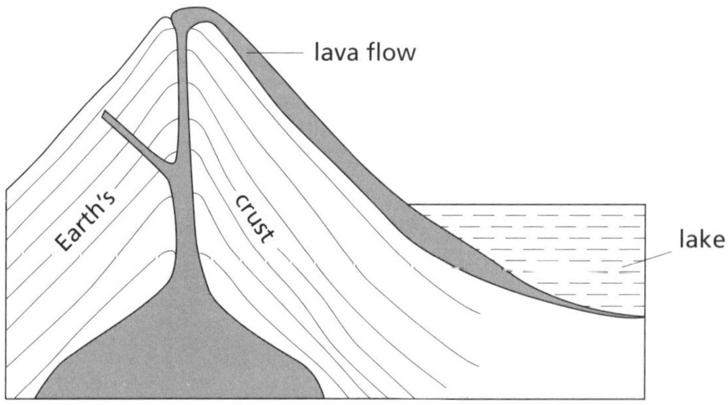


(a) Explain why igneous rocks may contain bubbles and crystals of different sizes.

.......................................................................................................................

.......................................................................................................................

....................................................................................................................... (3)

(b) Why do different compounds separate as different layers in the lake?

..............................................................................................................................

.............................................................................................................................. (3)

(c) What is the driving force of the rock cycle?

.............................................................................................................................. (1)

(d) Outline three processes which cause rocks to be weathered.

1 ..........................................................................................................................

2 ..........................................................................................................................

3 .......................................................................................................................... (3)

(e) Describe the processes which take place to turn an igneous rock into a metamorphic rock.

..............................................................................................................................

.............................................................................................................................. (3)

**3** (a) Millions of years ago the atmosphere of the Earth contained carbon dioxide with some ammonia, methane and water vapour. At that time the surface temperature of the Earth was very high.

(i) What was the surface temperature of the Earth when the water vapour began to condense and form the seas and oceans?

.............................................................................................................................. (1)

(ii) All the water we use comes from the oceans and seas by what is known as the water cycle. Label the arrows in the diagram by choosing the correct words.
**condensation evaporation precipitation** Each word should only be used once.

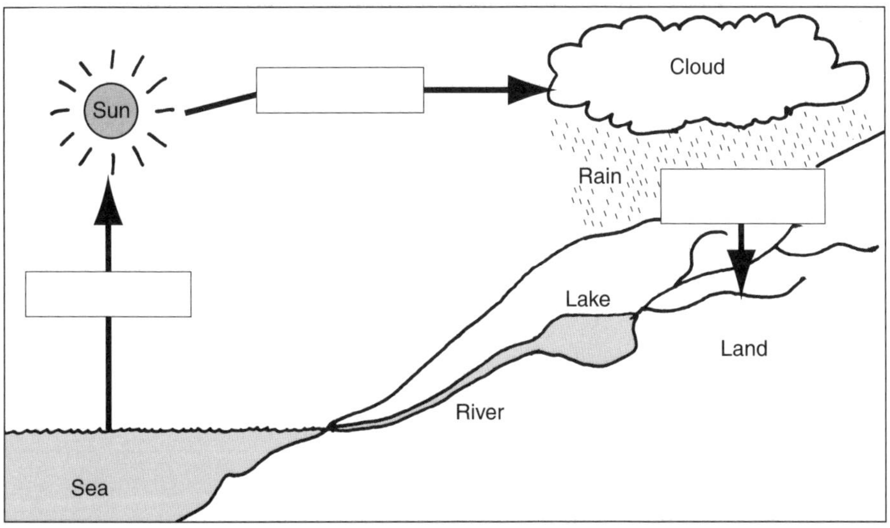


(2)

QUESTIONS

(b) Today's atmosphere still contains small amounts of carbon dioxide and water vapour. Complete the table by writing in the missing information about the two main gases in the air.

| Name of gas | Amount in air |
|---|---|
| | 78% |
| oxygen | |

(2)

(c) The action of plate tectonic processes causes the recycling of rocks.

(i) State **one** natural occurrence, often disastrous, that can happen at a plate boundary.

........................................................................................................................ (1)

(ii) Use the diagram to explain how each of the following changes occurs.

- magma forms igneous rock
- igneous rock becomes part of sedimentary rock
- sedimentary rock becomes metamorphic rock
- metamorphic rock becomes magma

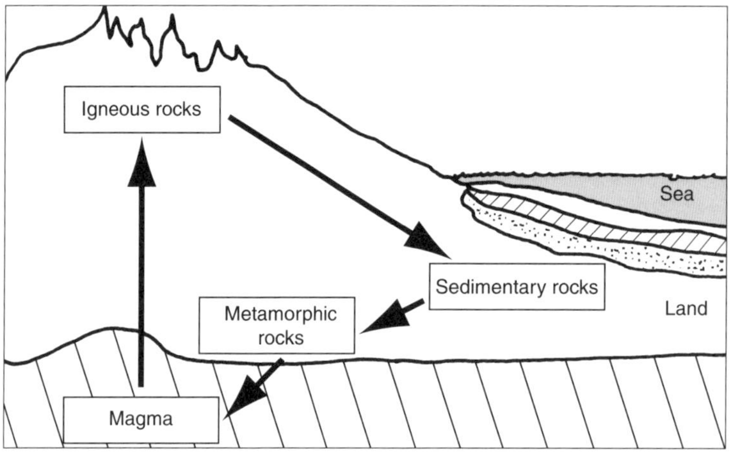


........................................................................................................................

........................................................................................................................

........................................................................................................................

........................................................................................................................ (4)

*SEG 1998*

**4** (a) Lead is extracted from lead(II) sulphide. Lead(II) sulphide is roasted in air to produce lead(II) oxide and sulphur dioxide gas. The lead(II) oxide is then heated in a blast furnace with coke (carbon).

(i) Write an equation for the reaction of lead(II) sulphide and oxygen.

........................................................................................................................ (2)

(ii) Explain why it would be damaging to the environment to allow the sulphur dioxide to escape into the atmosphere.

..........

..........

..........

.......... (2)

(iii) Suggest why lead extraction plants are sometimes sited near to chemical works where sulphuric acid is made.

..........

.......... (1)

(b) The equation for the reaction which occurs when lead(II) oxide is heated in a blast furnace with coke is given below.

$$2PbO + C \rightarrow 2Pb + CO_2$$

(i) What type of chemical process does the lead(II) oxide undergo in this reaction?

.......... (1)

(ii) Assuming that a tonne of coke contains 90% of usable carbon, calculate how much coke is needed to extract the lead from 10 tonnes of lead(II) oxide.

..........

..........

..........

..........

.......... (5)

(c) The lead contains about 1.2 kg of silver per tonne of lead. The silver is removed by adding about 2% of zinc to molten lead in a furnace at about 800 K.

Here is some data to consider.

The melting point of lead is 601 K; the melting point of zinc is 693 K.
Zinc is less dense than lead.
Zinc and lead do not mix when molten.
Silver is much more soluble in molten zinc than in molten lead.
Silver-zinc mixtures have much higher melting points than either pure zinc or pure lead.
Silver-zinc mixtures are less dense than molten lead.

QUESTIONS

(i) Write **true** or **false** after each of these statements.

The silver will dissolve mostly in the zinc ..........................................................

A silver-lead mixture will form on top of the zinc ..............................................

Lead will float on top of a silver-zinc liquid mixture ..........................................

A silver-zinc mixture will form on top of molten lead .......................................... (2)

(ii) Why do you think so much trouble is taken to remove such a small amount of silver from each tonne of lead?

..........................................................................................................................

.......................................................................................................................... (1)

(d) Here is some data about some salts.

| | |
|---|---|
| lead(II) chloride | insoluble in cold water (20° C)<br>soluble in hot water |
| lead(II) nitrate | soluble in hot and cold water |
| sodium chloride | soluble in hot and cold water |

(i) Starting from lead(II) nitrate and sodium chloride, describe how you would obtain some well-shaped crystals of lead(II) chloride.
Include essential practical details and give an equation for any reaction taking place.

..........................................................................................................................

..........................................................................................................................

..........................................................................................................................

..........................................................................................................................

..........................................................................................................................

..........................................................................................................................

.......................................................................................................................... (4)

(ii) Why does the reaction of lead(II) oxide and cold hydrochloric acid stop very quickly?

..........................................................................................................................

.......................................................................................................................... (1)

*MEG 1996*

QUESTIONS

5 Zinc occurs in the Earth's crust mainly as zinc sulphide, ZnS.
The flow chart shows the main steps in extracting the metal.

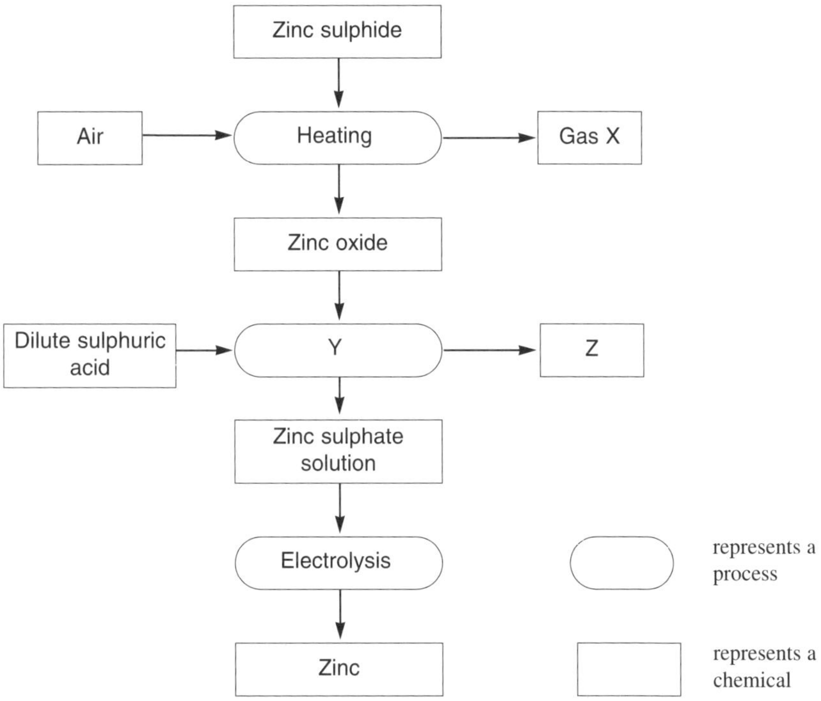


(a) Gas X is a possible cause of acid rain pollution.
Suggest a name for X.

.......................................................................................................... (1)

(b) (i) What name is given to the type of reaction (Y) taking place between zinc oxide and dilute sulphuric acid?

.......................................................................................................... (1)

(ii) Name the other product, Z, of this reaction.

.......................................................................................................... (1)

(c) The zinc sulphate solution is electrolysed and zinc metal forms at the negative electrode.
Write the ion-electron equation for the formation of zinc metal.
(You may wish to use your data booklet.)

.......................................................................................................... (1)

(d) Give a use for zinc metal.

.......................................................................................................... (1)

*SQA 1997*

# Air and atmosphere

## REVISION SUMMARY

**NORMAL COMPOSITION OF DRY AIR (by volume)**

| | |
|---|---|
| nitrogen | 78.1% |
| oxygen | 21.0% |
| argon | 0.9% |
| carbon dioxide | 0.03% |
| Traces of neon krypton xenon | |

Air is a mixture of gases. The most common gas in the air is nitrogen and this is very unreactive. The active gas in the air is oxygen. The composition of the air varies but a typical composition of air is: nitrogen 78.1 %; oxygen 21.0 %; argon 0.09 %; carbon dioxide 0.03 %; traces of neon, krypton and xenon.

The gases in the air can be separated by fractional distillation of liquid air. Liquid air is allowed to warm up and nitrogen boils off before oxygen because it has a lower boiling point. Oxygen has a wide range of uses, including for breathing equipment and in steel making. Much of the nitrogen produced is turned into fertilisers. Noble gases, such as argon, are very unreactive and are used to fill light bulbs.

Processes such as combustion, rusting and respiration use up oxygen in the air. Green plants replace oxygen by the process of photosynthesis. These processes are summarised in the carbon cycle.

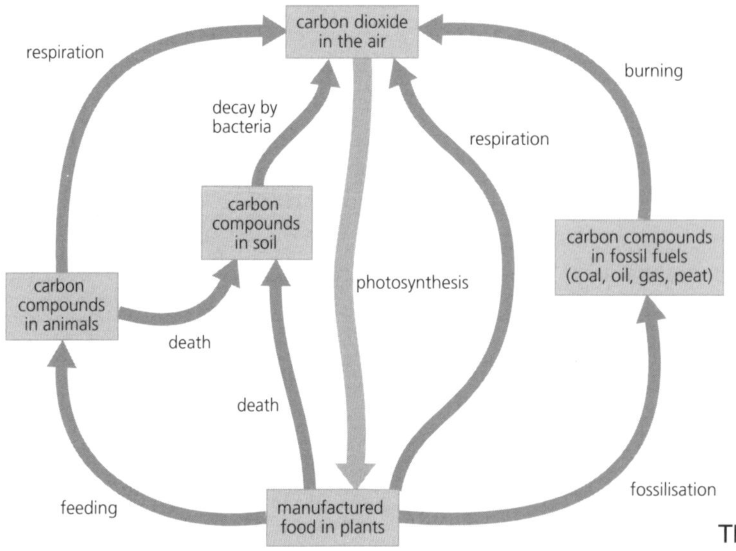


The carbon cycle

### Air pollution

The normal composition of air is given above on the left. Other gases get into the air and can alter the volume composition of air. Probably the most serious pollutant of air has been sulphur dioxide, which is produced when fuels containing sulphur are burned. Coal, in particular, contains appreciable amounts of sulphur and so produces sulphur dioxide on combustion. When sulphur dioxide gets into the air, it is oxidised, and, in the presence of water, produces sulphuric acid. It is probably the most important cause of **acid rain**. Acid rain makes lakes and rivers too acidic, killing off fish and other water-life, causes the death of trees and vegetation, the erosion of stonework and the corrosion of metal. As the amount of sulphur dioxide in the atmosphere is being reduced, as a result of restrictions on the burning of coal, desulphurisation processes in coal-fired power stations and the use of other means of generating electricity, the levels of another pollutant are becoming dangerously high. This is nitrogen oxide, which is produced, along with carbon monoxide, in car exhausts. Many of the effects of nitrogen oxide are similar to those of sulphur dioxide.

Burning fuels containing carbon efficiently to produce carbon dioxide has problems. As we burn more of these fuels, the levels of carbon dioxide in the atmosphere are increasing. This produces the **greenhouse effect**, where energy from the Sun reaches the Earth and cannot be re-radiated. As a result, the temperature of the Earth is rising and this will have effects on climate.

The use of chlorofluorocarbons (CFCs) as refrigerants and in aerosol sprays is now being controlled, as these chemicals, when they are released into the atmosphere, destroy the **ozone layer** in the upper atmosphere. It is the ozone layer that shields the Earth from the most powerful ultraviolet rays from the Sun.

**If you need to revise this subject more thoroughly, see the relevant topics in the *Letts GCSE Chemistry Study Guide*, or *CD-ROM*.**

QUESTIONS

**1** This question is about the process of photosynthesis which goes on in green plants.

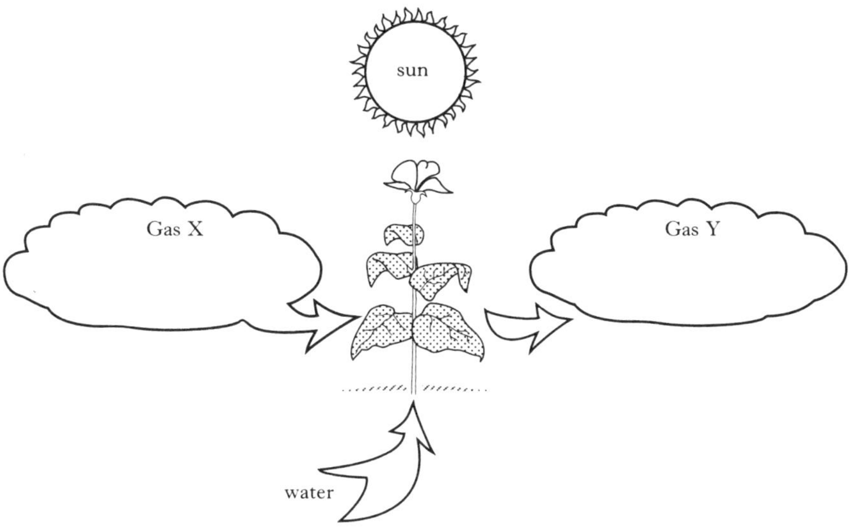


(a) Write down the names of the gases X and Y in the diagram.

Gas X ..............................................................................................................

Gas Y .............................................................................................................. (1)

(b) Explain the job of photosynthesis in keeping the composition of the atmosphere constant.

..............................................................................................................

.............................................................................................................. (2)

*SQA 1995*

**2** A scientist analysed the fumes emitted from a factory chimney.
The fumes contained these substances.

**carbon dioxide**
**carbon monoxide**
**carbon particles**
**sulphur dioxide**
**water**

(a) Which substance in the list causes most global warming?

.............................................................................................................. (1)

(b) Methane is a gas which also causes global warming.
Name **one** source of methane pollution.

.............................................................................................................. (1)

QUESTIONS

(c) Five years after the factory was built, the stonework of a building nearby started to crumble.

Suggest how the factory might have caused this.

..........................................................................................................................

..........................................................................................................................

.......................................................................................................................... (2)

(d) The graph shows the average levels of sulphur dioxide in the atmosphere.

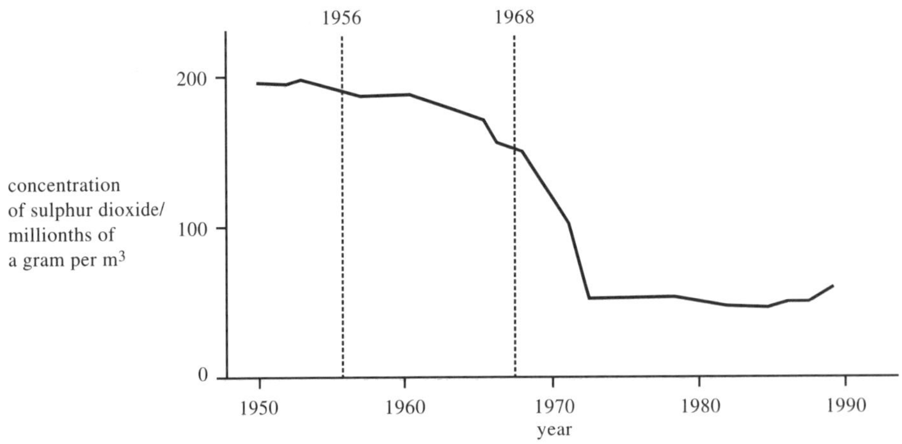


New laws about air pollution were passed in 1956 and 1968.

What evidence is there that the 1968 law had more effect than the 1956 law?

..........................................................................................................................

..........................................................................................................................

.......................................................................................................................... (2)

*MEG 1995*

**3** The table gives some information about the physical properties of five carbon compounds.

| Name | Formula | Melting point (°C) | Boiling point (°C) | Density as a liquid (g per cm³) |
|---|---|---|---|---|
| Cyclohexene | $C_6H_{10}$ | −103 | 83 | 0.81 |
| Dichlorodifluoromethane | $CCl_2F_2$ | −158 | −30 | 1.40 |
| Ethane | $C_2H_6$ | −183 | −89 | 0.57 |
| Methane | $CH_4$ | −182 | −164 | 0.47 |
| Propane | $C_3H_8$ | −190 | −42 | 0.58 |

Use the data to help you answer the following questions.

(a) Which of the compounds has the lowest melting point?

.................................................................................................................................... (1)

(b) Dichlorodifluoromethane is a chlorofluorocarbon (CFC). CFCs are liquids under pressure. They vaporise rapidly when the pressure is reduced to atmospheric pressure. CFCs can be used as propellants in aerosol sprays.

(i) Draw a diagram to show the arrangement of outer electrons in a molecule of dichlorodifluoromethane.

(2)

(ii) What type of bonding exists in a molecule of dichlorodifluoromethane?

.................................................................................................................................... (1)

(iii) Why is there concern about the quantities of CFCs being released into the atmosphere?

....................................................................................................................................

....................................................................................................................................

.................................................................................................................................... (3)

(iv) Which one of the compounds in the table would you choose as an alternative to dichlorodifluoromethane in aerosol sprays? Give your reasons.

Compound ..........................................................................................................................

Reasons .............................................................................................................................. (2)

# 5 Quantitative chemistry

REVISION SUMMARY

Understanding quantitative aspects of chemistry is important on papers at higher levels. The following important terms need to be understood.

### Relative atomic mass, $A_r$

This is the number of times the mass of one atom of an element is heavier than the mass of one-twelfth of a carbon-12 atom (or approximately the mass of a hydrogen atom).

### The mole

A mole is the amount of substance which contains $6 \times 10^{23}$ particles (Avogadro's number). 1 mole of copper, for example, contains the same number of particles as 1 mole of sulphur atoms and twice as many particles as 0.5 moles of magnesium. The mass of 1 mole of an element or a compound can be found using relative atomic masses.

E.g. mass of 1 mole of (a) copper, Cu; (b) oxygen atoms, O; (c) oxygen molecules, $O_2$; (d) calcium carbonate, $CaCO_3$; (e) calcium hydroxide, $Ca(OH)_2$.

(a) $A_r(Cu) = 64$. Mass of 1 mole of copper atoms = 64 g.

(b) $A_r(O) = 16$. Mass of 1 mole of oxygen atoms = 16 g.

(c) Mass of 1 mole of oxygen *molecules* = 32 g.

(d) $A_r(Ca) = 40$, $A_r(C) = 12$, $A_r(O) = 16$.
Mass of 1 mole of calcium carbonate = $40 + 12 + (3 \times 16) = 100$ g.

(e) $A_r(Ca) = 40$, $A_r(O) = 16$, $A_r(H) = 1$.
Mass of 1 mole of calcium hydroxide = $40 + 2(16 + 1) = 74$ g.

You can calculate the number of moles of a substance by dividing the mass of the substance by the mass of 1 mole.

### Molar volume

One mole of molecules of any gas occupies a volume of 24 $dm^3$ at room temperature and atmospheric pressure.

### Molar solution

A solution containing 1 mole of solute dissolved to make 1 $dm^3$ of solution is called a molar solution (M solution). A 2M solution contains 2 moles of solute in each cubic decimetre of solution.

### Empirical formula

This is the simplest formula of a compound in which the atoms are in the correct ratio. $CH_2$ is the empirical formula for $C_2H_4$, $C_3H_6$, $C_4H_8$, etc. To get the molecular formula it is necessary to know the mass of 1 mole (or relative molecular mass).

The formula of a compound can be obtained from the reacting masses of the reactants.

E.g. 6.0 g of carbon combines with 1.0 g of hydrogen.

Converting into numbers of moles:

6.0/12 moles of carbon atoms combines with 1.0/1 moles of hydrogen atoms.
0.5 moles of carbon atoms combines with 1 mole of hydrogen atoms.
Empirical formula is $CH_2$.
If the mass of 1 mole is 28 g, the molecular formula is $C_2H_4$.

The formula of a compound can be obtained in a similar way from percentages. If you are told that a compound of only iron, sulphur and oxygen contains 28% iron and 24% sulphur, you could work out the percentage of oxygen by difference. It is the same as the previous calculation, but using 28 g Fe, 24 g S, and 48 g O.

REVISION SUMMARY

The percentage of an element present in a compound can be found from the mass of the element present and the mass of 1 mole of the compound. For example, the percentage of nitrogen in ammonium nitrate, $NH_4NO_3$, can be found if we know that $A_r$(N) = 14, $A_r$(H) = 1, $A_r$(O) = 16.

Mass of 1 mole of ammonium nitrate = 14 + 4 + 14 + (3 × 16) = 80 g.
Mass of nitrogen present = 2 × 14 g.
Percentage of nitrogen = 100 × 28/80 = 35%.

Balanced symbolic equations can be used for calculating the quantities of reacting substances and products. The equation:

$$\text{E.g. } CaCO_3 + 2HCl \rightarrow CaCl_2 + H_2O + CO_2$$

tells us that 1 mole of calcium carbonate (100 g) combines with 2 moles of hydrochloric acid (71 g or 2 $dm^3$ of M solution) to form 1 mole of calcium chloride (111 g) and 1 mole of water (18 g) and 1 mole of carbon dioxide (44 g). Note the sum of the masses of the reactants always equals the sum of the masses of the products.

**Calculating the concentration of a solution**

What is the molar concentration of a solution of hydrochloric acid containing 7.3 g of hydrogen chloride in 100 $cm^3$ of solution? ($A_r$(H) = 1, $A_r$(Cl) = 35.5)

Mass of 1 mole of hydrogen chloride, HCl, = 1 + 35.5 = 36.5 (Unit 6)

7.3 g of hydrogen chloride in 100 $cm^3$ of solution has the same molar concentration as 73 g of hydrogen chloride in 1000 $cm^3$ of solution. The solution contains 73/36.5 moles of hydrogen chloride. The solution is 2 M (or 2 moles/$dm^3$).

A solution of known concentration is called a **standard solution**. Using a standard solution of hydrochloric acid, the concentration of a sodium hydroxide solution can be found by titration. The symbolic equation:

$$NaOH(aq) + HCl(aq) \rightarrow NaCl(aq) + H_2O(l)$$

tells us that 1 mole of sodium hydroxide reacts with 1 mole of sodium hydroxide. The hydrochloric acid is put into a burette. Exactly 25 $cm^3$ of sodium hydroxide solution is added to a conical flask using a pipette, and a couple of drops of screened methyl orange (or other suitable indicator) is added to the contents of the flask. The solution is now green. Hydrochloric acid is added from the burette until the solution just goes violet. This is called the **end point**. The solution is now neutral. Adding extra acid now would change the indicator pink. The volume of acid added can now be recorded and the process repeated.

**If you need to revise this subject more thoroughly, see the relevant topics in the Letts GCSE *Chemistry Study Guide*, or *CD-ROM*.**

QUESTIONS

1 (a) The reaction on mixing solutions of sodium hydroxide and hydrochloric acid is shown.

$$NaOH + HCl \rightarrow NaCl + H_2O$$

Write the balanced ionic equation for this reaction.

.......................................................................................................................... (2)

(b) Varying amounts of sodium hydroxide solution and hydrochloric acid were mixed, but the total volume of the mixture was always 50 $cm^3$. The temperatures of the solutions before and after mixing were recorded. A graph of the results is shown.

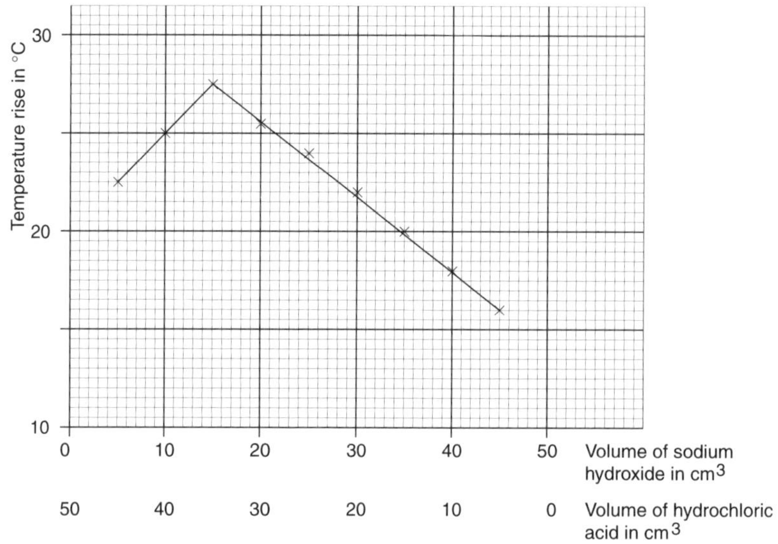


(i) What was the highest temperature rise?

.......................................................................................................................... (1)

(ii) Explain how the highest temperature rise shows that the sodium hydroxide solution has a higher concentration than the hydrochloric acid solution.

..........................................................................................................................

.......................................................................................................................... (2)

(c) Calculate the concentration in mol/$dm^3$ of a solution that was made by dissolving 100 g of sodium hydroxide and making the solution up to 1.0 $dm^3$.
Relative atomic masses: H = 1; O = 16; Na = 23.

..........................................................................................................................

..........................................................................................................................

..........................................................................................................................

Concentration of sodium hydroxide solution = ................................................ mol/$dm^3$ (3)

Letts Q&A

(d) Calculate the total mass of sodium chloride that can be made from 100 g of sodium hydroxide.
Relative atomic masses: H = 1; O = 16; Na = 23; Cl = 35.5.

.................................................................................................................................

.................................................................................................................................

.................................................................................................................................

.................................................................................................................................

Mass of sodium chloride = ............... g (3)

(e) Sodium can be made from the electrolysis of molten sodium chloride. Explain why sodium and molten sodium chloride conduct electricity in different ways.

.................................................................................................................................

.................................................................................................................................

.................................................................................................................................

................................................................................................................................. (2)

*SEG 1998*

**2** This question concerns the electrolysis of molten calcium bromide, $CaBr_2$, using carbon electrodes.

(a) Draw a labelled diagram of the apparatus used for the electrolysis of molten calcium bromide. Include a switch and a bulb in your circuit.

(3)

QUESTIONS

(b) A current of 5 A is passed for 193 seconds.

(i) How many coulombs of electricity have passed?

........................................................................................................................ (2)

(ii) How many Faradays of electricity have passed? (1 Faraday = 96 500 coulombs)

........................................................................................................................ (1)

(iii) Calcium is produced at the negative electrode by the discharge of $Ca^{2+}$ ions. How many moles of calcium atoms were produced?

........................................................................................................................ (2)

(iv) Bromine is produced at the positive electrode by the discharge of $Br^-$ ions. How many moles of bromine atoms were produced at the positive electrode?

........................................................................................................................ (2)

(c) At the end of the experiment the heat was removed and the calcium bromide turned solid. The bulb continued to glow. Explain.

........................................................................................................................

........................................................................................................................ (1)

(d) When the apparatus was washed up at the end of the experiment, bubbles of colourless gas were produced. What was the colourless gas and how was it formed?

........................................................................................................................

........................................................................................................................ (3)

**3** Washing soda is hydrated sodium carbonate, $Na_2CO_3xH_2O$. An experiment was carried out to find the value of $x$.

28.6 g of fresh hydrated sodium carbonate crystals were dissolved in distilled water and the solution made up to a volume of 1000 $cm^3$. 25 $cm^3$ of this solution was transferred to a conical flask and a few drops of methyl orange indicator added.

The solution in the conical flask was titrated with 0.25 M hydrochloric acid (0.25 mole/$dm^3$) and 20.0 $cm^3$ of acid were required to reach the end point.

(a) Name the most suitable piece of apparatus for measuring out exactly 25 $cm^3$ of sodium carbonate solution and transferring it to the conical flask.

........................................................................................................................ (1)

QUESTIONS

(b) How would you know that the end point of the titration had been reached?

........................................................................................................................ (1)

(c) Write a balanced symbolic equation for the reaction of sodium carbonate with dilute hydrochloric acid.

........................................................................................................................ (2)

(d) How many moles of hydrochloric acid react with 25 $cm^3$ of sodium carbonate solution?

(2)

(e) How many moles of hydrochloric acid would react with 1000 $cm^3$ of sodium carbonate solution?

(2)

(f) Using the equation, how many moles of anhydrous sodium carbonate are present in 1000 $cm^3$ of sodium carbonate solution?

(2)

(g) What mass of anhydrous sodium carbonate is present in 1000 $cm^3$ of sodium carbonate solution? ($A_r$(Na) = 23, $A_r$(C) = 12, $A_r$(O) = 16)

(2)

(h) Complete the following:

................. g of anhydrous sodium carbonate combines with ................. g of water to produce 28.6 g of sodium carbonate crystals. (1)

(i) How many grams of water would combine with 1 mole of sodium carbonate?

........................................................................................................................ (1)

(j) What is the value of $x$? ($A_r$(H) = 1, $A_r$(O) = 16)

........................................................................................................................ (1)

QUESTIONS

**4** Toners for colouring black-and-white photographs are made by mixing two solutions. The solutions should be made up using warm water.

| Solution 1 |
|---|
| Sodium sulphide solution concentration 100 g/l |

| Solution 2 |
|---|
| Sodium hydroxide solution concentration 80 g/l |

(a) Why is **warm** water used to make up the solutions?

........................................................................................................................ (1)

(b) Calculate the concentration of sodium hydroxide in mol/l.
**Show your working clearly.**

(2)

(c) Different colours are obtained by mixing the two solutions.

| Colour | Volume of sodium sulphide solution/$cm^3$ | Volume of sodium hydroxide solution/$cm^3$ |
|---|---|---|
| cold brown | 10 | 40 |
| brown | 20 | 30 |
| warm brown | 30 | 20 |

What mass of sodium sulphide will be required to make 100 $cm^3$ of toner for a cold brown colour? **Show your working clearly.**

(2)

*SQA 1995*

**5** Limestone is impure calcium carbonate. The purity can he found by adding a measured amount of limestone to a measured, excess of dilute hydrochloric acid. The following reaction takes place.

$$CaCO_3(s) + 2HCl(aq) \rightarrow CaCl_2\,(aq) + H_2O(l) + CO_2\,(g)$$

(a) (i) State TWO methods by which you could tell that pure calcium carbonate had completely reacted with dilute hydrochloric acid.

1 ........................................................................................................................

........................................................................................................................

2 ........................................................................................................................

........................................................................................................................ (2)

QUESTIONS

(ii) One of these methods is not reliable with impure samples of calcium carbonate such as limestone. State which ones and give a reason for its unreliability.

..................................................................................................................

.................................................................................................................. (1)

(b) After the limestone has reacted, sodium hydroxide can then be added to neutralise the remaining excess acid. The following reaction takes place.

$NaOH(aq) + HCl\ (aq) \rightarrow NaCl\ (aq) + H_2O\ (l)$

Write the ionic equation for this reaction.

.................................................................................................................. (2)

(c) In a determination of the percentage purity of limestone, the following results were obtained.

| | | |
|---|---|---|
| Mass of hydrochloric acid in solution | = | 20.00 g |
| Mass of limestone | = | 25.00 g |
| Mass of hydrochloric acid left unreacted | = | 2.48g |

(i) What mass of hydrochloric acid reacted with the limestone?

.................................................................................................................. (1)

(ii) Using the equation

$CaCO_3\ (s) + 2HCl\ (aq) \rightarrow CaCl_2\ (aq) + H_2O\ (l) + CO_2\ (g)$

calculate the mass of calcium carbonate with which this mass of hydrochloric acid would react.

..................................................................................................................

..................................................................................................................

..................................................................................................................

..................................................................................................................

.................................................................................................................. (4)

(iii) Calculate the percentage purity of the limestone (the percentage of pure calcium carbonate in the limestone).

..................................................................................................................

.................................................................................................................. (1)

*Edexcel 1995*

# 6 The Periodic Table

**REVISION SUMMARY**

The Periodic Table is an arrangement of chemical elements in order of increasing atomic number. Elements with similar properties are in the same vertical column (or group). The horizontal rows are called **periods**.

The Periodic Table was first devised by the Russian chemist Mendeleef in 1869. You will have a copy of this table in your examination to help you. Use this table to check the spelling of the element name, the symbol, the mass number, the atomic number and elements with similar properties. For example, if you want to know about the chemistry of silicon, you will notice it is in the same group as carbon and this should help you write the formula of its oxide as $SiO_2$, similar to $CO_2$.

The table consists of eight groups of elements in the **main block**. These are Groups I to VII and 0.

Group I elements are called the alkali metals and Group VII elements are called the halogens. You need to know the chemistry of these two groups. Group 0 elements are called the noble gases. Between the two parts of the main block are the elements called **transition metals**. These include iron, nickel and copper.

Metals are on the left-hand side of the table and non-metals on the right-hand side. There is often a bold stepped line to divide metals from non-metals. Elements which are gases at room temperature and atmospheric pressure, are in the top right-hand corner of the table.

Elements with similar chemical properties, i.e. in the same group, have similar outer electron arrangements, e.g. lithium 2,1 and sodium 2,8,1. Apart from the noble gases, the number of electrons in the outer energy level of any element in the main group is the same as the group number of the element.

The table gives the electron arrangement of the first 20 elements in the Periodic Table and the formulae of oxides and chlorides of these elements.

| Element | Electron arrangement | Formula of oxide | Formula of chloride |
|---|---|---|---|
| hydrogen | 1 | $H_2O$ | HCl |
| helium | 2 | ------ | --------- |
| lithium | 2,1 | $Li_2O$ | LiH |
| beryllium | 2,2 | BeO | $BeH_2$ |
| boron | 2,3 | $B_2O_3$ | $B_2H_6$ |
| carbon | 2,4 | $CO_2$ | $CH_4$ |
| nitrogen | 2,5 | range | $NH_3$ |
| oxygen | 2,6 | ------ | $H_2O$ |
| fluorine | 2,7 | $F_2O$ | HF |
| neon | 2,8 | ----- | ---- |
| sodium | 2,8,1 | $Na_2O$ | NaH |
| magnesium | 2,8,2 | MgO | $MgH_2$ |
| aluminium | 2,8,3 | $Al_2O_3$ | $AlH_3$ |
| silicon | 2,8,4 | $SiO_2$ | $SiH_4$ |
| phosphorus | 2,8,5 | $P_2O_5$ | $PH_3$ |
| sulphur | 2,8,6 | $SO_3$ | $H_2S$ |
| chlorine | 2,8,7 | $Cl_2O_7$ | HCl |
| argon | 2,8,8 | ------ | ---- |
| potassium | 2,8,8,1 | $K_2O$ | KH |
| calcium | 2,8,8,2 | CaO | $CaH_2$ |

**If you need to revise this subject more thoroughly, see the relevant topics in the *Letts GCSE Chemistry Study Guide*, or *CD-ROM*.**

QUESTIONS

1 Use the Periodic Table to help you answer the following questions.
(a) 0.46 g of sodium combines with oxygen to form 0.62 g of an oxide of sodium.
Use this information to find the empirical formula of this oxide of sodium.

.......................................................................................................................

.......................................................................................................................

.......................................................................................................................

....................................................................................................................... (4)

(b) (i) Complete the diagrams below to show the electronic structures of a sodium atom and an oxygen atom.

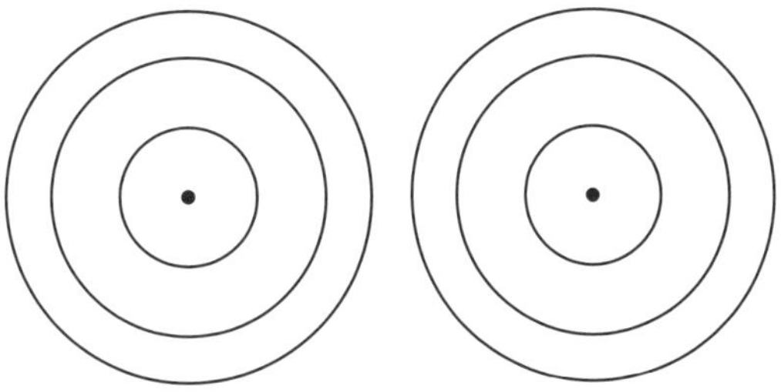


(2)

(ii) Describe the formation of sodium oxide in terms of transfer of electrons between sodium and oxygen atoms.

.......................................................................................................................

.......................................................................................................................

....................................................................................................................... (4)

(c) Describe what you **see** when sodium metal reacts with water.

.......................................................................................................................

.......................................................................................................................

....................................................................................................................... (2)

(d) (i) Give the electronic structure of an argon atom.

(1)

Letts Q&A

(ii) Use the electronic structure of an argon atom to help you to explain why the noble gases like argon are monatomic and unreactive.

..........................................................................................................................

..........................................................................................................................

..........................................................................................................................

.......................................................................................................................... (2)

*NEAB 1998*

**2** This diagram shows part of the Periodic Table.
The letters do **not** represent the symbols for the elements.

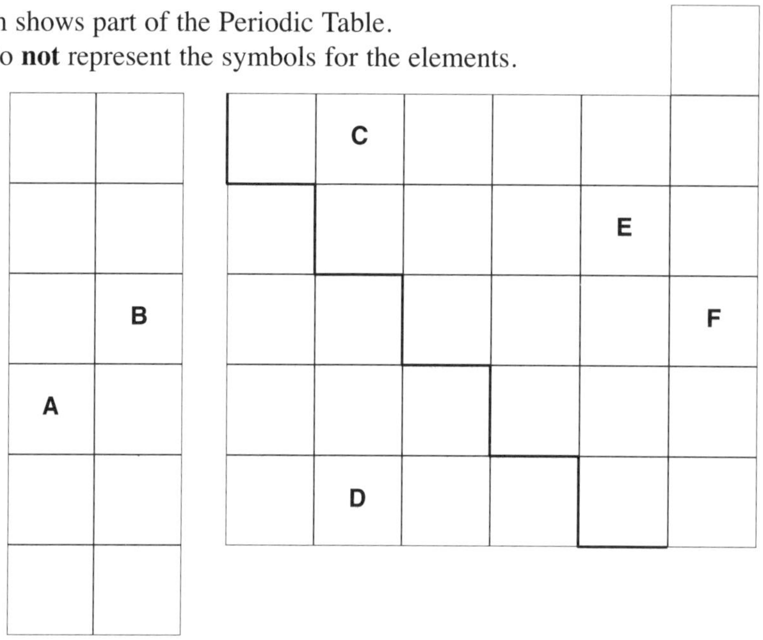


(a) Identify the alkali metal.

| | | | | | |
|---|---|---|---|---|---|
| A | B | C | D | E | F |

(1)

(b) Identify the element which exists as diatomic molecules.

| | | | | | |
|---|---|---|---|---|---|
| A | B | C | D | E | F |

(1)

(c) Identify the **two** elements which are in the same group.

| | | | | | |
|---|---|---|---|---|---|
| A | B | C | D | E | F |

(1)

*SQA 1995*

**3** The table below gives some of the properties of elements in group II of the Periodic Table

| Element | Symbol | Reaction with water | Formula of chloride |
|---|---|---|---|
| Beryllium | Be | | $BeCl_2$ |
| ***Magnesium*** | Mg | Reacts slowly with cold water, vigorously with steam | $MgCl_2$ |
| ***Calcium*** | Ca | Reacts steadily with cold water | $CaCl_2$ |
| ***Strontium*** | Sr | Reacts vigorously with cold water | $SrCl_2$ |
| ***Barium*** | Ba | Reacts very vigorously with cold water | |

(a) Arrange the **four** elements in ***italics*** in order of reactivity, putting the most reactive first.

.................................................................................................................................... (1)

(b) Suggest what would happen when beryllium is added to cold water.

....................................................................................................................................

.................................................................................................................................... (1)

(c) Suggest how barium should be safely stored.

....................................................................................................................................

.................................................................................................................................... (1)

(d) When barium is heated in chlorine gas they react to form a solid.

(i) Give the name and formula of the solid formed.

Name ...........................................................................................................................

Formula ....................................................................................................................... (2)

(ii) Describe the bonding in the compound.

...........................................................................................................................

...........................................................................................................................

........................................................................................................................... (3)

# 7 Rates of reaction

**REVISION SUMMARY**

Some chemical reactions are finished in a tiny fraction of a second and some can take millions of years. A reaction which takes place in a very short period of time is called a **fast** reaction. One which takes place over a long period of time is called a **slow** reaction.

The burning of a mixture of hydrogen and oxygen with a squeaky pop is a very fast reaction. The rusting of a steel fence is much slower and the reactions turning vegetable matter into crude oil much slower still. The rate of a chemical reaction can be altered by changing the conditions of the reaction. The souring of milk can be slowed by cooling the milk in a refrigerator.

## Factors which speed up a chemical reaction include:

1. Increasing temperature. As an approximation, in many chemical reactions, a 10° C temperature rise doubles the rate of reaction.
2. Increasing the concentration of one or more of the reactants. In the reaction of sodium thiosulphate and dilute hydrochloric acid, doubling the concentration of sodium thiosulphate doubles the rate of the reaction. You must be careful as this relationship, of doubling the rate of a reactant, doubling the rate of the reaction, is not true in all cases.
3. Using a catalyst. A catalyst alters the rate of a chemical reaction without being used up. Usually a catalyst speeds up a reaction. Some catalysts, called negative catalysts or inhibitors, slow down reactions. A common example of a catalyst is manganese(IV) oxide in the decomposition of hydrogen peroxide into water and oxygen.
4. Using one of the reactants in a more finely powdered form. For example, powdered calcium carbonate reacts much faster with dilute hydrochloric acid than a lump of calcium carbonate of the same mass.
5. Using light. A mixture of hydrogen and chlorine explodes in sunlight, but does not in the dark. Light can provide the initial energy needed to start a reaction. This is called the **activation energy**.
6. Increasing pressure. This can increase the speed of a reaction involving gases.

## Explaining the rate of reaction in a simple particle theory

You should be able to explain changes in the rate of a chemical reaction in terms of numbers of successful collisions of reacting particles. Increasing the temperature of a reaction mixture speeds up the particles and results in more collisions between particles. It will also result in more collisions where the particles have sufficient energy to react and so the reaction is speeded up.

Increasing the concentration will again result in more particle collisions and therefore the reaction is faster.

A catalyst provides an alternative route for the reaction which needs a lower activation energy. More collisions have this lower energy and so the reaction is faster.

When one of the reactants is powdered, a large surface area is provided. As a result, there are more collisions and, so, more successful collisions.

Light works in a similar way to heating: providing additional energy and increasing the pressure is the same as increasing the concentration.

## Enzymes

Enzymes are **biological** catalysts which control important processes such as fermentation. An enzyme is a protein. Enzymes work only with certain reactions and under certain conditions. For example, catalase will catalyse the decomposition of hydrogen peroxide but at high temperatures the structure of the enzyme is permanently changed (denatured) and it will no longer work.

**If you need to revise this subject more thoroughly, see the relevant topics in the Letts GCSE *Chemistry Study Guide*, or *CD-ROM*.**

**1** John investigated the reaction of calcium carbonate with hydrochloric acid. The same mass of calcium carbonate and the same volume of acid were used in each experiment.

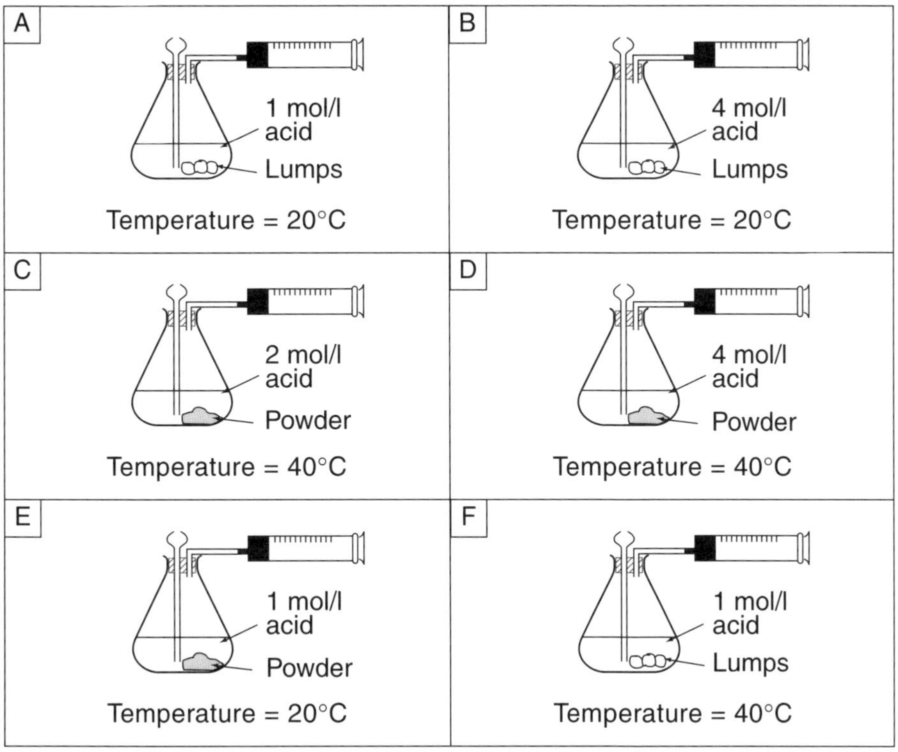


(a) Identify the experiment in which gas was produced most quickly.

| | | | | | |
|---|---|---|---|---|---|
| **A** | **B** | **C** | **D** | **E** | **F** |

(1)

(b) Identify the **two** arrangements which would have been compared to show the effect of particle size on the rate of the reaction.

| | | | | | |
|---|---|---|---|---|---|
| **A** | **B** | **C** | **D** | **E** | **F** |

(1)

*SQA 1995*

**2** The decomposition of hydrogen peroxide is catalysed by manganese(IV) oxide.

$$2H_2O_2(aq) \rightarrow 2H_2O(l) + O_2(g)$$

Two experiments were carried out by a student.
The first experiment used small lumps of the catalyst.
The results of this experiment using the small lumps are shown in the table.

QUESTIONS

| Time (min) | 0 | 0.5 | 1.0 | 1.5 | 2.0 | 2.5 | 3.0 | 3.5 | 4.0 | 4.5 |
|---|---|---|---|---|---|---|---|---|---|---|
| Volume of oxygen ($cm^3$) | 0 | 18 | 24 | 48 | 58 | 63 | 73 | 78 | 80 | 80 |

(a) (i) Select a suitable scale for each axis, and plot these values on the grid below. Draw a smooth curve, allowing for any anomalous result.

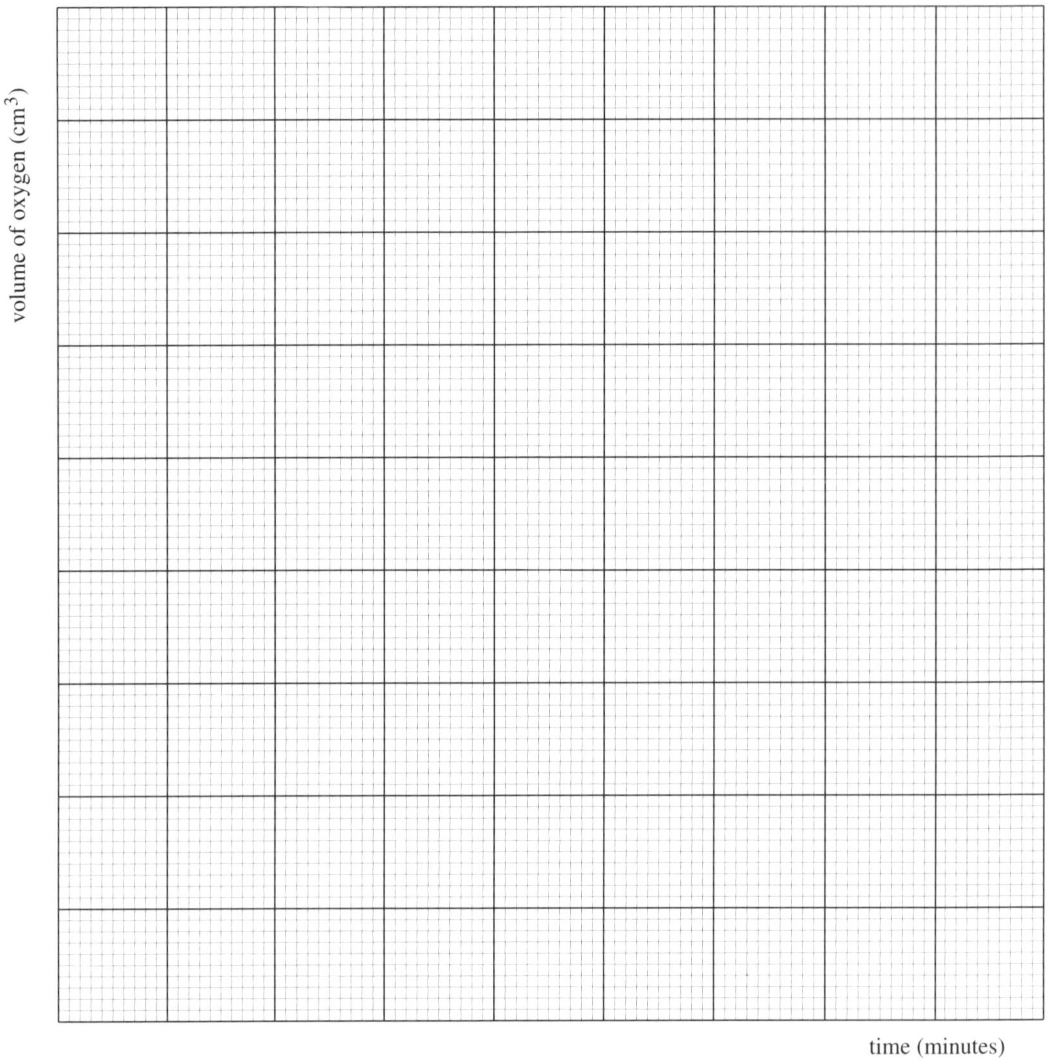


(3)

(ii) Explain, in terms of particles, why the rate of reaction was faster at the beginning of the experiment.

..............................................................................................................................

..............................................................................................................................

.............................................................................................................................. (2)

(b) The experiment was repeated using powdered catalyst.
All other conditions were kept the same.
On the grid, sketch a curve to show the results you would expect for this experiment. (2)

*NEAB 1998*

REVISION SUMMARY

There are some very important industrial processes involving chemical reactions. In Unit 2 processes of fractional distillation, cracking and polymerisation were considered, whilst the extraction of aluminium and iron were considered in Unit 3. In this Unit two more processes are considered, the manufacture of ammonia by the Haber process and the manufacture of sulphuric acid by the Contact process.

In any question involving an industrial process you are not required to know the technical details of the process. You are required to:

- know the raw materials required and all the products formed;
- understand the chemical principles involved in the process;
- be able to evaluate social, economic, health and safety, and environmental factors associated with the process.

## Contact process for making sulphuric acid

The Contact process is a three-stage process for producing sulphuric acid, probably the most important industrial chemical, from sulphur or sulphur-containing minerals.

In stage 1, the sulphur or sulphur-containing mineral is burnt in air to form sulphur dioxide.

$$S + O_2 \rightarrow SO_2$$

In stage 2, sulphur dioxide and oxygen react together to produce sulphur trioxide.

$$2SO_2 + O_2 \rightleftharpoons 2SO_3$$

This is a reversible reaction, which means that 100% conversion of the reactants into products is impossible. In such a situation an **equilibrium** is set up, where the rate of the forward reaction and the rate of the reverse reaction are the same and the concentrations of the reactants and products remain unchanged. The economic success of the process will depend upon getting the equilibrium to 'move as far as possible to the right', i.e. to get conditions which produce an equilibrium with a high concentration of sulphur trioxide. The optimum conditions are a temperature of about 450°C and a catalyst of vanadium(V) oxide.

In stage 3, the sulphur trioxide is dissolved in concentrated sulphuric acid to produce oleum (fuming sulphuric acid) which is then diluted with the required amount of water to make concentrated sulphuric acid.

$$SO_3 + H_2SO_4 \rightarrow H_2S_2O_7$$
$$H_2S_2O_7 + H_2O \rightarrow 2H_2SO_4$$

This is preferable to dissolving the sulphur trioxide directly into water.

## Haber process for making ammonia

In the Haber process, nitrogen and hydrogen are combined together to form ammonia. Again the reaction is reversible and conditions must be established to get the equilibrium established as far to the right as possible.

$$N_2 + 3H_2 \rightleftharpoons 2NH_3 \qquad \text{Forward reaction exothermic}$$

Nitrogen and hydrogen are mixed together in the proportions of 1 part of nitrogen and 3 parts of hydrogen. The mixture is compressed to a high pressure and passed over a catalyst of finely divided iron at a temperature of about 450°C.

The best conditions are *high pressure* (there are more molecules on the left-hand side of the equation than on the right and increasing pressure moves the equilibrium to the right) and *low temperature*. (As the forward reaction is exothermic, lowering the reaction temperature moves the equilibrium to the right. However, lowering the temperature slows down the rate of reaction: using a catalyst helps to speed up the reaction, but does not affect the position of the equilibrium.) Even under these favourable conditions only about 10% of the nitrogen and hydrogen are converted into ammonia. The unreacted gases are recycled.

The ammonia gas is cooled and liquified to remove it from the other gases. Most of the ammonia is used to make nitric acid or nitrogeneous fertilisers.

**If you need to revise this subject more thoroughly, see the relevant topics in the Letts GCSE *Chemistry Study Guide*, or *CD-ROM*.**

QUESTIONS

1 The flow diagram refers to processes used in manufacturing important ammonium compounds.

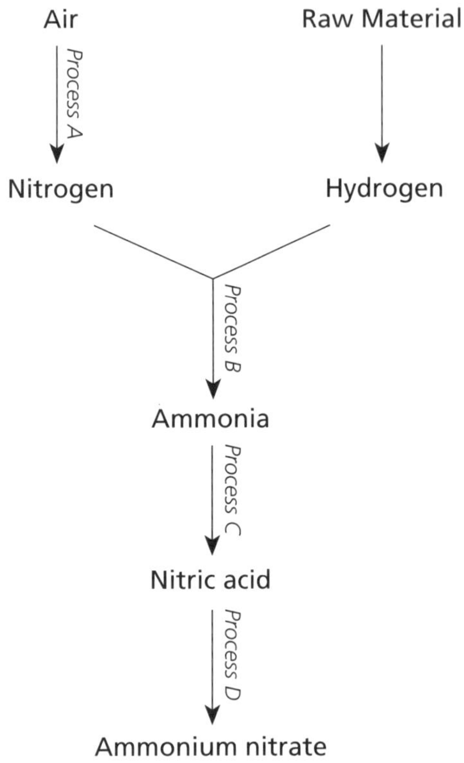


(a) Give the name of:

(i) Process A ..................................................................

(ii) Process B ..................................................................

(iii) Process D .................................................................. (3)

(b) What is the major use of ammonium nitrate?

.................................................................................................................................... (1)

(c) What are the conditions for process B?

....................................................................................................................................

....................................................................................................................................

.................................................................................................................................... (3)

(d) Process C involves a three-stage process for converting ammonia into nitric acid.

Stage 1: Ammonia is mixed with air and the mixture is passed over a heated platinum gauze catalyst. Nitrogen monoxide and steam are produced.

$$4NH_3(g) + 5O_2(g) \rightarrow 4NO(g) + 6H_2O(g)$$

Stage 2: The mixture of gases is cooled and nitrogen dioxide is formed.

$$2NO(g) + O_2(g) \rightarrow 2NO_2(g)$$

Stage 3: The nitrogen dioxide is dissolved in water.

$$4NO_2(g) + 2H_2O(l) + O_2(g) \rightarrow 4HNO_3(l)$$

(i) The platinum gauze has to be heated to start the reaction, but then heating is not necessary. What does this tell you about Stage 1?

.................................................................................................................... (1)

(ii) What mass of nitric acid could be produced from 17 tonnes of ammonia? ($A_r$(H) = 1, $A_r$(N) = 16, $A_r$(O) = 16)

....................................................................................................................

.................................................................................................................... (2)

**2** (a) Limestone is mined in County Armagh, very close to the ancient Navan Fort.

(i) What is the chemical name for limestone?

.................................................................................................................... (1)

(ii) Give **two** advantages and **two** disadvantages which can arise from limestone quarrying.

....................................................................................................................

....................................................................................................................

....................................................................................................................

....................................................................................................................

.................................................................................................................... (4)

(b) The uses of metals are linked to their properties.
Complete the table below which shows the uses and properties of some metals.

| Metal | Property | Use |
|---|---|---|
| aluminium | | manufacture of saucepans |
| copper | very unreactive | |
| | low melting point | in solder |

(3)

QUESTIONS

(c) The manufacture of iron in the blast furnace illustrates different types of chemical reactions.

(i) Balance the equation below which shows the reduction of an iron ore, magnetite, by carbon monoxide.

$Fe_3O_4 + CO \rightarrow Fe + CO_2$ (1)

(ii) Which chemical is **oxidised** in the above reaction?

.......................................................................................................................... (1)

(iii) Which substance in the blast furnace undergoes thermal decomposition?

.......................................................................................................................... (1)

(d) (i) All living things contain the radioactive isotope carbon-14 which undergoes beta decay. Complete the nuclear equation below to show what happens when carbon-14 undergoes beta decay.

$^{14}_{6}C \rightarrow \qquad + \qquad$ (2)

(ii) A very old wooden boat was found to contain only 25% of the carbon-14 which is present in a living tree. The half life of carbon-14 is 5730 years. How long ago was the wood cut down to make the boat? Show your working.

Answer = ......................................... (2)

*NICCEA 1998*

Water is a compound of hydrogen and oxygen. The atoms are held together in the water molecule by covalent bonds.

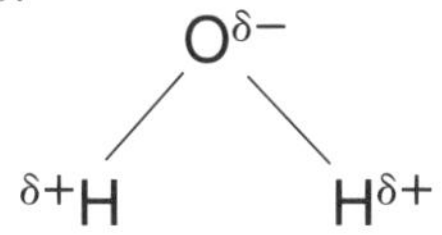


Water exists in three states: ice, liquid water and water vapour. The changes of state occur at O° C and 100° C The boiling point of water is higher than expected because of extra forces holding the molecules together. These are called **hydrogen bonds**.

Water is an extremely good solvent. It dissolves a wide range of different solutes. Usually the solubility of gases in water decreases with increasing temperature. The solubility of solid solutes usually increases with increasing temperature. A graph showing the change in solubility with temperature is called a **solubility curve**. The **solubility** of a solute is the maximum mass of the solute which will dissolve in 100 g of water at a particular temperature.

## Water supplies

Because water is a very good solvent, it is difficult to get and keep pure. Even as rainwater falls to Earth it dissolves carbon dioxide in the atmosphere and is no longer pure water. When rainwater falls on calcium carbonate rocks, some of the rock reacts with the rainwater.

$$CaCO_3(s) + H_2O(l) + CO_2(g) \rightleftharpoons Ca(HCO_3)_2(aq)$$

This water now contains **temporary hardness**, which can be removed by boiling. If rainwater falls on rocks containing calcium sulphate or magnesium sulphate, they dissolve slightly and the resulting water contains **permanent hardness**, which cannot be destroyed by boiling. Hard water does not lather well with soap but forms a scum. It lathers well with soapless detergents. Permanent hardness can be removed by treatment with chemicals such as washing soda (hydrated sodium carbonate) or the use of ion-exchange resins.

As it is very difficult to get pure water, no attempt is made to deliver pure water to our homes through a water main. Suitable clean supplies of water are filtered to remove any solid impurities and treated with chlorine to kill any harmful bacteria.

Water pollution is caused by chemicals entering streams and rivers. Many of these chemicals come from farmland, where fertilisers, pesticides, etc. wash off the fields and build up in the water. Nitrogen compounds from sewage and animal waste or from excess fertilisers are a particular problem. Oxidation of ammonia to nitrates uses up the dissolved oxygen in the water. Fish need the oxygen for respiration. Nitrogen and phosphorus compounds in water also encourage the growth of water plants, which prevent light from entering the water. Even nitrates, which were once thought not to be a serious problem have now been shown to be harmful, particularly when in high concentrations in drinking water for babies. Industry can also cause problems, especially if very harmful heavy metals such as lead or cadmium are allowed to escape into rivers.

Sea water is a source of chemicals. Apart from salt which is obtained by evaporation in warmer countries, the sea provides most of the world's supply of magnesium and bromine. Bromine is obtained by acidifying sea water and then bubbling chlorine through it to liberate bromine, which is then obtained by fractional distillation.

$$2NaBr + C1_2 \rightarrow 2NaCI + Br_2$$

## Testing for ions

Analysis means the breaking up into smaller units and is the opposite of **synthesis**. In chemistry we may carry out **qualitative analysis** to find out what is present.

**Carbonate $CO_3^{2-}$**

When dilute hydrochloric acid is added to a carbonate, carbon dioxide gas is produced. The carbon dioxide turns limewater milky. No heating is required.

REVISION SUMMARY

**Chloride $Cl^-$**

When a solution of a chloride is acidified with dilute nitric acid and silver nitrate solution is added, a white precipitate of silver chloride is formed immediately This precipitate turns purple in sunlight and dissolves completely in concentrated ammonia solution.

**Sulphate $SO_4^{2-}$**

When dilute hydrochloric acid and barium chloride solution are added to a solution of a sulphate, a white precipitate of barium sulphate is formed immediately.

**Nitrate $NO_3^-$**

If sodium hydroxide solution is added to a solution of a nitrate and then aluminium powder is added, a reaction takes place on gentle warming. Hydrogen gas is produced from the reaction of the aluminium and sodium hydroxide. However, if a nitrate is present, ammonia gas is also produced which turns damp red litmus paper blue.

**Ammonium $NH_4^+$, Aluminium $Al^{3+}$, Copper(II) $Cu^{2+}$, Iron(II) $Fe^{2+}$, Iron(III) $Fe^{3+}$**

These cations can be identified with tests using sodium hydroxide solution. If an ammonium ion is heated with sodium hydroxide solution, ammonia gas is produced.

If sodium hydroxide is added dropwise to solutions of aluminium, copper(II), iron (II) and iron(III) the following results are obtained.

| | |
|---|---|
| Aluminium | White precipitate of aluminium hydroxide is formed, which dissolves in excess sodium hydroxide. |
| Copper(II) | A pale blue precipitate of copper(II) hydroxide is formed. |
| Iron(II) | A dirty green precipitate of iron(II) hydroxide is formed. |
| Iron(III) | A red-brown precipitate of iron(III) hydroxide is formed. |

**Salts**

Salts are compounds formed when a metal (or an ammonium group) replaces hydrogen in an acid. Salts can be divided into salts soluble in water and salts insoluble in water.

**Preparation of soluble salts**

Soluble salts are prepared by the reaction between an acid and a metal, metal oxide, metal hydroxide or metal carbonate,

e.g. $CuO(s) + H_2SO_4(aq) \rightarrow CuSO_4(aq) + H_2O(l)$.

The salt is recovered by evaporation of the solution until a small volume remains and then leaving it to cool and crystallise.

**Preparation of insoluble salts**

Insoluble salts are prepared by mixing solutions of appropriate chemicals so that the insoluble salt is formed by precipitation,

e.g. $AgNO_3(aq) + NaCl(aq) \rightarrow AgCl(s) + NaNO_3(aq)$.

The insoluble salt is removed by precipitation and washed and dried.

1 Information about the solubility of some barium salts is given below.

| Salt | | Solubility in water |
|---|---|---|
| barium carbonate | $BaCO_3$ | insoluble |
| barium chloride | $BaCl_2$ | soluble |
| barium nitrate | $Ba(NO_3)_2$ | soluble |
| barium sulphate | $BaSO_4$ | insoluble |

(a) (i) Barium carbonate reacts with dilute hydrochloric acid to form barium chloride solution.
What would you **see** during this reaction?

..........................................................................................................

.......................................................................................................... (2)

(ii) Write the balanced equation for this reaction.

.......................................................................................................... (2)

(iii) Barium chloride solution is used to test for the presence of sulphate ions.
Write the balanced **ionic** equation for the reaction in this test.

.......................................................................................................... (2)

(b) Describe how you would prepare a sample of pure, dry barium sulphate from barium chloride crystals and dilute sulphuric acid.

..........................................................................................................

..........................................................................................................

.......................................................................................................... (3)

(c) Solutions containing barium ions are very poisonous and yet a 'barium meal' containing barium sulphate is given to some patients before taking X-rays of their stomachs.

(i) Explain why a 'barium meal' containing barium sulphate is not poisonous.

.......................................................................................................... (1)

(ii) The stomach contains hydrochloric acid. Explain why barium carbonate must not be substituted for barium sulphate in a 'barium meal'.

..........................................................................................................

.......................................................................................................... (1)

*Edexcel 1998*

QUESTIONS

2 Potassium nitrate, $KNO_3$, and ammonium sulphate, $(NH_4)_2SO_4$, are both used as artificial fertilisers.
(Relative atomic masses: H = 1.0, N = 14.0, O = 16.0, S = 32.0, K = 39.0.)

(a) Calculate the percentage of nitrogen in:

(i) potassium nitrate

..........................................................................................................

..........................................................................................................

.......................................................................................................... (2)

(ii) ammonium sulphate

..........................................................................................................

..........................................................................................................

.......................................................................................................... (2)

(b) Give TWO advantages of potassium nitrate over ammonium sulphate as a fertiliser.

1 ..........................................................................................................

..........................................................................................................

2 ..........................................................................................................

.......................................................................................................... (2)

(c) Both of the above fertilisers are soluble in water. Explain one environmental hazard of using too much of a soluble nitrogenous fertiliser on fields at any one time.

..........................................................................................................

..........................................................................................................

..........................................................................................................

..........................................................................................................

..........................................................................................................

.......................................................................................................... (3)

*Edexcel 1997*

**3** The solubility curve for potassium dichromate, is shown on the grid.

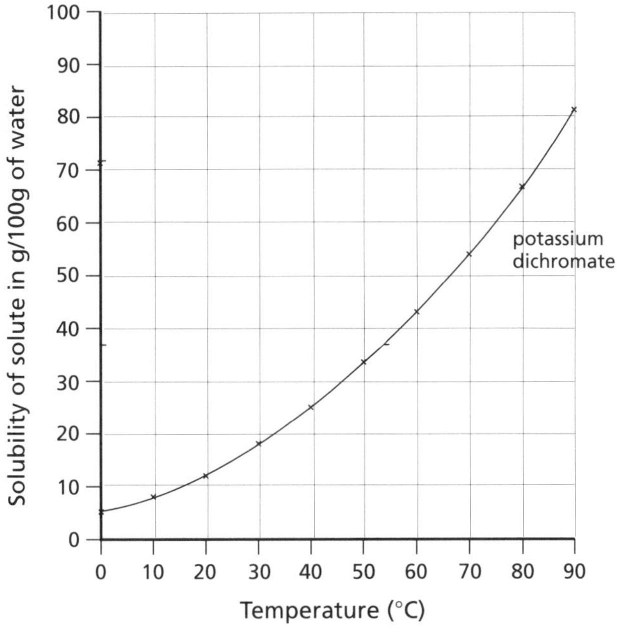


A student wanted to purify some potassium dichromate. She added some potassium dichromate to 100 g of water and heated gently while stirring. The compound just dissolved at 90° C. The solution was then allowed to cool to 50° C.

(a) What mass of potassium dichromate was added (ignore impurities)?

........................................................................................................................ (1)

(b) What mass of potassium dichromate would still be dissolved when the solution had cooled to 50° C?

........................................................................................................................ (1)

(c) What mass of crystals would be produced after the solution had stopped crystallising at 50° C?

........................................................................................................................ (1)

(d) How could the student obtain a sample of dry crystals of potassium dichromate from this experiment?

........................................................................................................................

........................................................................................................................ (2)

QUESTIONS

**4** The label on a bottle of mineral water had the following information.

| Ions present | | Concentration in g/litre |
|---|---|---|
| calcium | $Ca^{2+}$ | 0.10 |
| magnesium | $Mg^{2+}$ | 0.02 |
| sodium | $Na^{+}$ | 0.01 |
| potassium | $K^{+}$ | 0.01 |
| sulphate | $SO_4^{2-}$ | 0.14 |
| hydrogencarbonate | $HCO_3^{-}$ | 0.26 |

(a) (i) Name a compound which causes temporary hardness in this mineral water.

.................................................................................................................... (1)

(ii) Give one method that could be used to remove *permanent* hardness in water. Explain how this method works.

Method ....................................................................................................

....................................................................................................................

Explanation ..............................................................................................

.................................................................................................................... (3)

(b) Name the white solid deposit found in kettles which have been used to boil *temporarily* hard water.

.................................................................................................................... (1)

(c) Sodium stearate $C_{17}H_{35}COO^{-}Na^{+}$, is a soap. Explain how the scum is formed when this soap is used in hard water.

....................................................................................................................

....................................................................................................................

....................................................................................................................

.................................................................................................................... (3)

*SEG 1995*

Letts Q&A

*Time allowed:* ***1 hour and 15 minutes.***

**1** (a) The diagram shows a 'dot and cross' diagram for a hydrogen chloride molecule.

(i) What do each of the following represent?

● .............................. **O** ..............................

x .............................. • .............................. (4)

(ii) What type of bonding is shown in a molecule of hydrogen chloride?

.......................................................................................................................... (1)

(b) When hydrogen chloride is dissolved in water, each molecule is split into two ions.

(i) Draw 'dot and cross' diagrams to show the two ions formed.

(2)

(ii) Describe a test to show that a solution of hydrogen chloride in water contains ions.

..........................................................................................................................

.......................................................................................................................... (2)

(iii) Describe a test using an indicator to show that a solution of hydrogen chloride in water contains $H^+$ ions.

..........................................................................................................................

.......................................................................................................................... (2)

(c) When a solution of hydrogen chloride is added to a carbonate, bubbles of carbon dioxide gas are produced.

(i) Describe a test for carbon dioxide.

..........................................................................................................................

.......................................................................................................................... (2)

QUESTIONS

(ii) Finish an ionic equation for this reaction.

.................. + $CO_3^{2-}$ → $CO_2$ + .................. (2)

**2** (a) Finish the sentences by choosing the best words from this list.

**bubbles** **detergent** **magnesium** **scum** **soap** **sodium**

Water containing dissolved calcium and ........................ compounds is said to be hard water. Hard water does not lather well with ...................... , but forms ........................ . (3)

(b) In an experiment soap solution is added to 50 $cm^3$ samples of water until a lather is formed.
The table gives the volume of soap needed with different water samples.

| Sample | Volume of soap solution $cm^3$ |
|---|---|
| distilled water | 0.5 |
| P | 3.0 |
| Q | 5.0 |
| R | 4.0 |

(i) Name a piece of apparatus suitable for measuring out the water samples.

.................................................................................................................... (1)

(ii) Name a piece of apparatus suitable for adding the soap solution.

.................................................................................................................... (1)

(iii) Which solution contains most hardness?

.................................................................................................................... (1)

(c) The experiment is repeated using new samples of water. The water is boiled before the soap solution is added. The table gives the volume needed with each sample of boiled water.

| Sample | Volume of soap solution $cm^3$ |
|---|---|
| distilled water | 0.5 |
| P | 3.0 |
| Q | 4.0 |
| R | 0.5 |

What can be concluded about the hardness of each water sample P, Q and R from these experiments?

.......................................................................................................................................

.......................................................................................................................................

.......................................................................................................................................

.......................................................................................................................................

.......................................................................................................................................

....................................................................................................................................... (6)

(d) Finish the sentences by choosing the best words from this list.

**calcium carbonate** **calcium hydrogen carbonate** **calcium sulphate**
**sodium carbonate** **sodium chloride**

Temporary hardness is caused by dissolved ................................. . This is formed when

rocks containing ................................. are dissolved by rainwater.

Permanent hardness is caused by dissolved ................................. . Hard water can be

softened by using ................................. . (4)

3 Iron can form two chlorides.

(a) When chlorine gas is passed over heated iron, a brown iron chloride is formed.

| | | |
|---|---|---|
| Mass of iron weighed out | = | 1.50 g |
| Mass of iron remaining after the reaction | = | 0.38 g |
| Mass of iron chloride formed | = | 3.25 g |

(i) Calculate the mass of iron used in the reaction. ........................ g (1)

(ii) Calculate the number of moles of iron used. ($A_r(Fe) = 56$)

....................................................................................................................... (1)

(iii) Calculate the mass of chlorine combined in 3.25 g of iron chloride.

....................................................................................................................... (1)

QUESTIONS

(iv) Calculate the number of moles of chlorine used. ($A_r$(Cl) = 35.5)

.......................................................................................................... (1)

(v) Work out the formula of the brown iron chloride.

.......................................................................................................... (1)

(b) When hydrogen chloride is passed over heated iron, green iron chloride crystals are formed. Hydrogen is also formed.
5.6 g of iron reacts to form 12.7 g of green iron chloride.

(i) Show that the formula of green iron chloride is $FeCl_2$.

(3)

(ii) Write a balanced symbolic equation, with state symbols, for the reaction of iron and hydrogen chloride.

.......................................................................................................... (3)

(c) When sodium hydroxide solution is added to a solution of green iron chloride, $FeCl_2$, a green precipitate is formed. This precipitate goes darker on standing.
Explain the reactions taking place. Include equations in your answer.

..........................................................................................................

..........................................................................................................

..........................................................................................................

..........................................................................................................

.......................................................................................................... (5)

(d) Iron is a transition metal.
Write down three properties of iron which are typical of a transition metal.

1 ..........................................................................................................

2 ..........................................................................................................

3 .......................................................................................................... (3)

Letts Q&A

**4** Ethanol, $C_2H_5OH$, can be produced from ethene, $C_2H_4$.
Alternatively, it can be produced from sugar solution.

(a) The reaction of ethene to produce ethanol is an addition reaction.

(i) What is an addition reaction?

.................................................................................................................... (1)

(ii) Write a balanced equation for the reaction.

.................................................................................................................... (1)

(b) (i) Describe how aqueous ethanol can be prepared from sugar solution. Your answer should include the conditions required and a balanced symbolic equation.

....................................................................................................................

....................................................................................................................

....................................................................................................................

....................................................................................................................

....................................................................................................................

....................................................................................................................

....................................................................................................................

.................................................................................................................... (8)

(ii) How can a solution of ethanol be concentrated?
Explain what this method of separation depends upon.

....................................................................................................................

.................................................................................................................... (3)

(c) Ethanol is produced from sugar in Brazil. In Great Britain it is produced from ethene.
Suggest why different methods are used in these two countries.

....................................................................................................................

.................................................................................................................... (2)

QUESTIONS

**5** (a) The diagrams show the arrangement of particles in four substances.

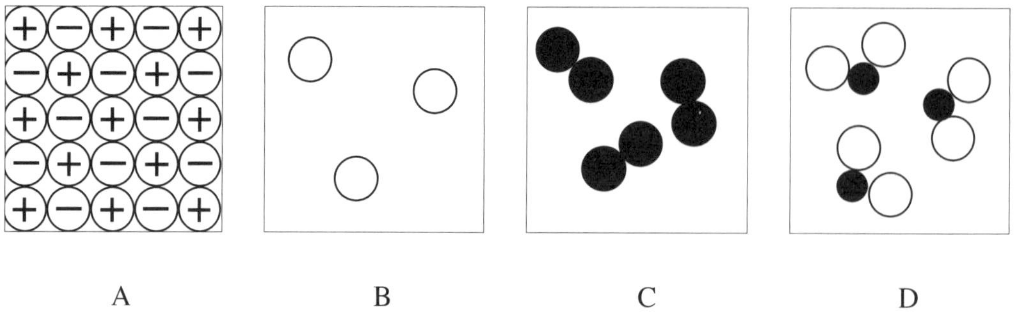


(i) Which diagram shows a noble gas? .................................................................. (1)

(ii) Which diagrams show elements? .................................................................. (2)

(iii) Which diagram shows an ionic compound? .................................................. (1)

(b) Silicon(IV) oxide, $SiO_2$, has a giant structure of atoms.
Sodium chloride, NaCl, has a giant structure of ions.
Iodine, $I_2$, has a molecular structure.

(i) Describe a test which you could use to decide whether a substance has a giant structure or a molecular structure.

..................................................................................................................

..................................................................................................................

.................................................................................................................. (3)

(ii) Describe a test which you could use to decide whether a substance with a giant structure is made up of atoms or ions.

..................................................................................................................

..................................................................................................................

.................................................................................................................. (3)

# Answers

## 1 STRUCTURE AND BONDING

| Question | | Answer | Mark |
|---|---|---|---|
| 1 | (a) | (i) hydrogen molecule (ii) chlorine molecule | 2 |

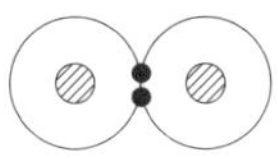

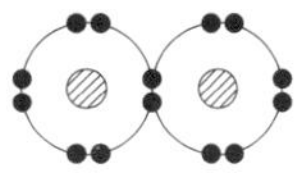

| Question | | Answer | Mark |
|---|---|---|---|
| | (b) | Covalent. | 1 |
| | (c) | Fluorine, chlorine and bromine molecules are similar. | 1 |
| | | Difference in mass: bromine heaviest, fluorine lightest. | 1 |
| | | Heavier molecules need more energy to move them and let them escape from the liquid. | 1 |
| | (d) | Hydrogen chloride (dry) contains a covalent bond. | 1 |
| | | On dissolving in water, the hydrogen chloride ionises *or* forms ions. | 1 |
| | | Ions are $H^+$ and $Cl^-$ *or better* show the electron arrangement in the ions. | 1 |

**Examiner's tip** You will frequently have to draw simple diagrams to represent atoms. In these diagrams it is usual only to show the nucleus and the outer electrons. If you attempt to show inner electrons incorrectly, you may lose marks. This question tests your understanding of covalent and ionic bonding. The change in the bonding of hydrogen chloride takes place when water is present.

| Question | | Answer | Mark |
|---|---|---|---|
| 2 | (a) | Isotopes. | 1 |
| | (b) | Because the relative atomic mass of lithium is 6.9 (closer to 7 than 6), most of the atoms present must be lithium-7. | 1 |

**Examiner's tip** This question is testing your understanding of the idea of isotopes. You are not expected to calculate the percentage of each isotope in the sample. You would be expected to do this at A level.

(c)

| Particle | Number |
|---|---|
| protons | 3 |
| neutrons | 4 |
| electrons | 2 |

Mark: 2

**Examiner's tip** Two marks are awarded in (c) if all three numbers are correct. One mark is awarded if two are correct. Be careful here. You are asked to work out the numbers of protons, neutrons and electrons in a lithium **ion**. Many candidates will work out the numbers of particles in a lithium atom.

| Question | | Answer | Mark |
|---|---|---|---|
| 3 | (a) | Motion is rapid and random. | 1 |
| | (b) | Particles possess more kinetic energy *or* move faster. | 1 |
| | | More collisions of particles with walls. | 1 |

| Question | Answer | Mark |
|---|---|---|

**Examiner's tip** Students frequently consider pressure as collisions between particles and not with the walls of the container.

| | | | | |
|---|---|---|---|---|
| | (c) | (i) | Sulphur. | 1 |
| | | (ii) | Diffusion. | 1 |
| | | (iii) | Hydrogen sulphide particles move about twice as fast as sulphur dioxide particles. | 1 |

**Examiner's tip** The ring of sulphur is closer to one end of the tube than the other. The ring would have formed in the middle if both moved with the same speed. Small (light) particles move faster than large (heavy) particles.

| | | | | |
|---|---|---|---|---|
| | | (iv) | The movement of particles is random and not in one direction only. | 1 |
| | | | Particles of air slow the movement of particles down the tube. | 1 |
| **4** | (a) | (i) | D | 1 |

**Examiner's tip** Melting point below 20° C, boiling point above 20° C.

(ii) E **1**

**Examiner's tip** Lowest density or is a gas.

(iii) A **1**

**Examiner's tip** Burns to form a basic oxide.

(iv) A **1**

**Examiner's tip** Density less than 1.0 g/cm$^3$ (density of water).

(v) F **1**

**Examiner's tip** Conductor when molten and dissolves in water.

(vi) B or C **1**

**Examiner's tip** B is preferred as it is a non-conductor – no chance of ions.

(b) (i) Allotropes (or polymorphs). **1**

**Examiner's tip** This question is a data handling question. You do not need a great deal of knowledge. You have to use the information given. Allotropes are often confused with isotopes or isomers.

(ii) They have the same boiling point. **1**

| Question | Answer | Mark |
|---|---|---|

**Examiner's tip** Both form acidic oxides, but they could still be different non-metallic elements.

| | (iii) | They form acidic oxides. | 1 |
|---|---|---|---|

## 2 OIL AND CARBON CHEMISTRY

| Question | | | Answer | Mark |
|---|---|---|---|---|
| 1 | (a) | | (You might need to refer to Unit 5.) | |
| | | | Percentage of oxygen = 50%. | 1 |
| | | | 37.5 g of C combines with 12.5 g of H and 50 g of O. | |
| | | | 37.5/12 moles of C combines with 12.5/1 moles of H and 50/16 moles of O. | 1 |
| | | | 3.125 moles C, 12.5 moles H, 3.125 moles O. | 1 |
| | | | Empirical formula is $CH_4O$. | 1 |
| | (b) | | 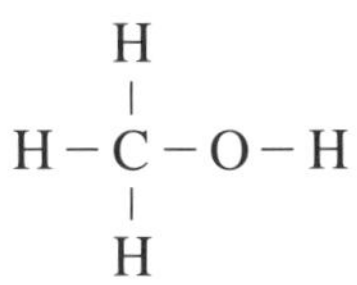 methanol | 1 |
| | (c) | | Alcohols (or alkanols). | 1 |
| | (d) | | Methanoic acid HCOOH. | 1 |

**Examiner's tip** The oxidation of an alcohol produces an acid. An homologous series is a family of similar compounds with the same general formula. The general formula of alcohols is $C_nH_{2n+1}OH$.

| Question | | | Answer | Mark |
|---|---|---|---|---|
| 2 | (a) | (i) | Crude oil is vaporised and vapour is cooled. | 1 |
| | | | Different compounds condense at different temperatures. | 1 |
| | | (ii) | Alkanes are hydrocarbons **or** compounds of carbon and hydrogen only | 1 |
| | | | that are saturated **or** with a general formula $C_nH_{2n+2}$. | 1 |
| | | (iii) | $CH_4 + 2O_2 \rightarrow CO_2 + 2H_2O$ | 3 |

**Examiner's tip** Here one mark is for knowing that the products are carbon dioxide and water, one mark for writing all four chemical formulae correctly and one mark for balancing. You do not need to add state symbols as these were not asked for.

| Question | | | Answer | Mark |
|---|---|---|---|---|
| | (b) | (i) | Cracking involves passing the vapour over a catalyst. | 1 |
| | | | The catalyst is heated. | 1 |
| | | (ii) | Bromine water. | 1 |
| | | | Turns from red to colourless. | 1 |

**Examiner's tip** It is important to give the colour before and after.

**Question** **Answer** **Mark**

(c) (i)

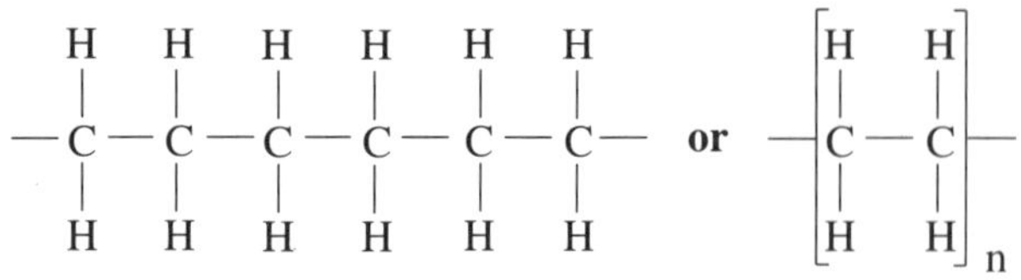

1

**Examiner's tip** It is important that the structure you draw shows two things.
1. The polymer molecule is very long.
2. The double bond between the two carbon atoms becomes a single bond.

(ii) Poly(ethene) 1

**Examiner's tip** Polythene is a trade name and you should give the chemical name.

(iii) Litter caused by plastic bags, bottles, etc. 1
Poly(ethene) does not react readily and therefore does not rot away. 1

**Examiner's tip** There may be other possible answers but you must state the problem caused for the first mark and then explain the problem for the second.

**3** (a) (i)

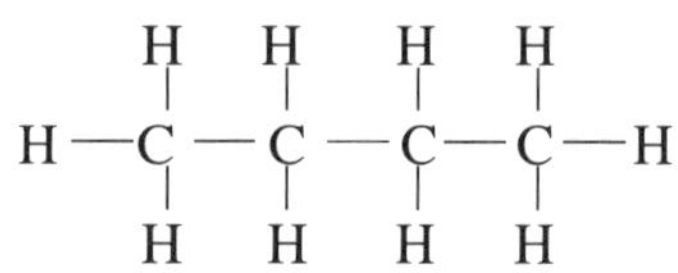

1

**Examiner's tip** There are two possible structures you could draw for butane. These are called isomers. Check you understand the terms isotope and allotrope, which are frequently confused with isomers (Unit 1). The other isomer is:

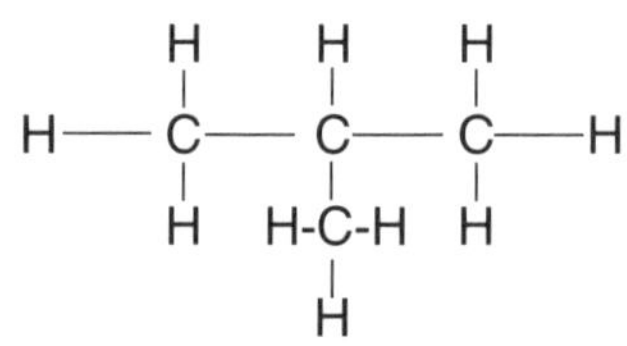

(ii)

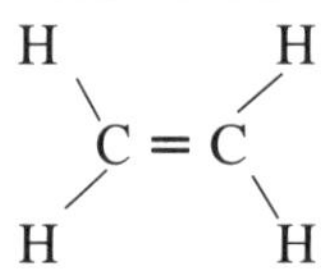

1

(b) (i) Reaction with ethene Bubble ethene through a solution of bromine at room temperature. 1

Reaction with butane Mix butane and bromine gases in sunlight. 1

(ii) Ethene Addition. 1

Butane Substitution. 1

(iii)

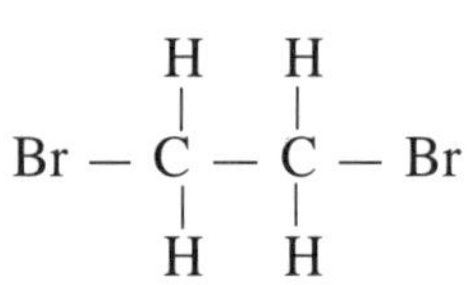

1

**Question** **Answer** **Mark**

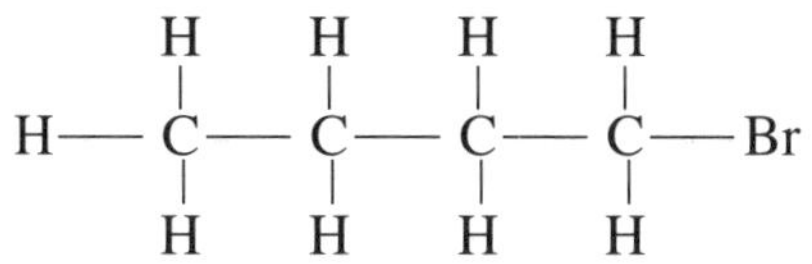

1

**Examiner's tip** The names of the two products are 1,2-dibromoethane and bromobutane. They are not required in your answer.

(c) (i) $2C_4H_{10}(g) + 13O_2(g) \rightarrow 8CO_2(g) + 10H_2O(l)$ **2**

**Examiner's tip** This is a very difficult equation to write. For one mark you must get the correct formulae for the two reactants and the two products. The second mark is for balancing the equation correctly.

(ii) From the equation 2 mole (48 $dm^3$) of butane needs (13 x 24) $dm^3$ of oxygen. **1**

Answer 1 $dm^3$ of butane needs 6.5 $dm^3$ of oxygen. **1**

**Examiner's tip** You will be given two marks for just writing down the answer. One mark will be deducted if you give no units.

**4** (a) (i) Alkanes. **1**

(ii) I. Complete combustion Carbon dioxide and water. **2**

II. Incomplete combustion Carbon monoxide and water. **2**

(b) (i) Reaction conditions for ethene and hydrogen,

140–180° C (or heat). **1**

Nickel catalyst. **1**

**Examiner's tip** Candidates are often vague about reaction conditions. Most reactions require heating.

Reaction of ethene and bromine water.

Product:

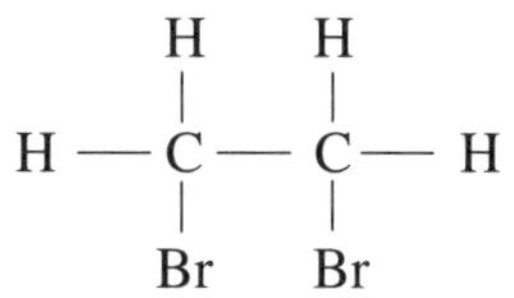

**Examiner's tip** The reaction of bromine water with ethene can produce 2-bromoethanol.

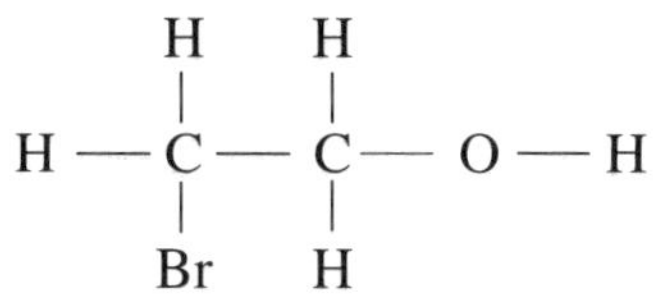

This must be accepted as a correct alternative answer.

| Question | | | Answer | Mark |
|---|---|---|---|---|
| | | | Reaction of ethene and water. | |
| | | | Conditions – bubble into concentrated sulphuric acid. | 1 |
| | | | Add water. | 1 |
| | | | Product: 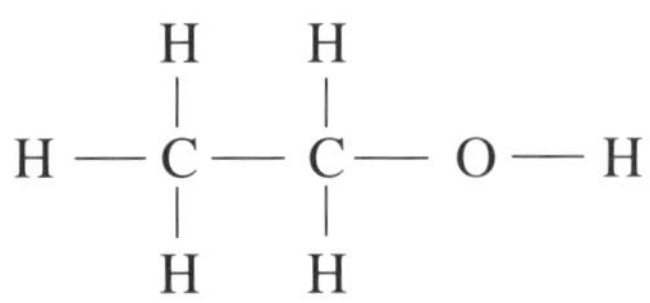 | |
| | | (ii) | Reaction with hydrogen. | 1 |
| | | (iii) | Natural fat or oil. | 1 |
| | (c) | (i) | 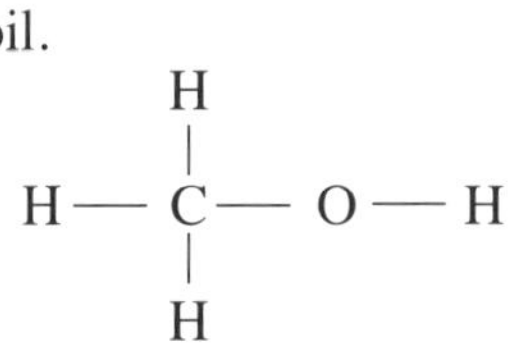 | 1 |
| | | (ii) | Reactant(s) Yeast and sugar solution,<br>Conditions 30–40° C, absence of air or oxygen.<br>Main by-product Carbon dioxide. (1 mark for each point) | 4 |
| | | (iii) | Uses include solvent, fuel, antifreeze and in thermometers. | 2 |

## 3 MATERIALS FROM ROCKS

| Question | | Answer | Mark |
|---|---|---|---|
| 1 | (a) | Average density is much greater than average density of any rocks of the crust, so there must be high density material in the Earth (core). | 1 |
| | (b) | 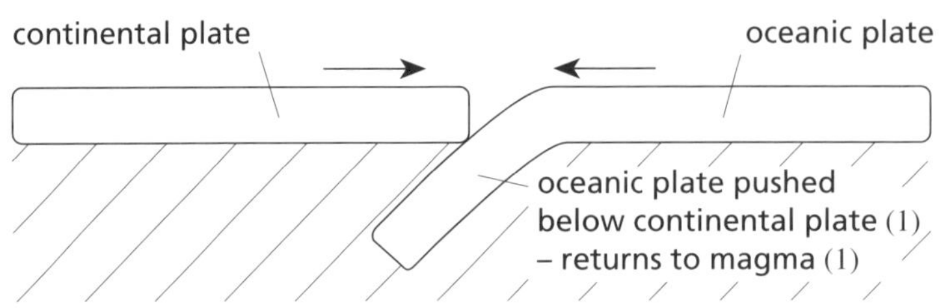 | 3 |

**Examiner's tip** There is one mark for the diagram and two for the labels. This is an example of where an annotated diagram is better than a lot of words.

| Question | | Answer | Mark |
|---|---|---|---|
| | (c) | Two plates rub together. | 1 |
| | | Stresses build up which when released produce earthquakes. | 1 |
| | (d) | Hot springs *or* volcanoes. | 1 |
| | (e) | South America and Africa were joined – hence similar rocks. | 1 |
| | | They have moved apart over a long period. | 1 |
| 2 | (a) | Bubbles caused by gases dissolved in magma. | 1 |
| | | Size of crystals dependent on rate of cooling. | 1 |
| | | Fast cooling – small crystals; slow cooling – large crystals. | 1 |

| Question | Answer | Mark |
|---|---|---|

**Examiner's tip** It is important to relate the size of crystals to the rate of cooling. When liquid magma cools and crystallises slowly, perhaps inside the Earth, large crystals form. When the magma cools and crystallises quickly, perhaps on the surface of the Earth, small crystals are formed.

| | | |
|---|---|---|
| (b) | Particles of different sizes (large particles deposited first). | 1 |
| | Different concentrations of dissolved materials. | 1 |
| | Different solubilities of dissolved materials. | 1 |
| (c) | Nuclear decay (radioactivity) processes in the Earth. | 1 |
| (d) | Any three of the following:<br>Freezing of water followed by thawing.<br>Wind.<br>Running water.<br>Chemical action due to carbon dioxide or sulphur dioxide.<br>Rubbing of one rock on another. | 3 |
| (e) | Erosion of rock. Transport of sediments. Deposition of sediments. Compaction of sediments to form sedimentary rock. Effect of high temperature. Effect of high pressure. | 3 |

**Examiner's tip** There are six points. Each counts for half a mark. The mark scored is rounded up if it contains a half mark. Be careful – answers such as temperature and pressure may not be acceptable without some qualification, e.g. high temperature or high pressure.

| | | |
|---|---|---|
| 3 (a) (i) | 100°C | 1 |
| (ii) | condensation<br>evaporation      precipitation | 2 |

**Examiner's tip** Here there are three answers but once you have two words in the correct places you automatically have the third. There are two marks for all three correct and one mark for two or one correct. The common mistake here is to get condensation and precipitation the wrong way round. You would then score 1.

| | | |
|---|---|---|
| (b) | nitrogen      20–21% | 2 |

**Examiner's tip** The percentage of oxygen must be less than 22% as we know there are significant amounts of other gases present, e.g. argon and carbon dioxide.

| | | |
|---|---|---|
| (c) (i) | Earthquakes. | 1 |
| (ii) | Igneous rock is formed when the magma crystallises. | 1 |
| | Igneous rocks are broken down by weathering and erosion, the sediments transported, deposited and cemented together to give sedimentary rocks. | 1 |
| | High temperatures and high pressures turn sedimentary rocks into metamorphic rocks. | 1 |
| | Metamorphic rocks melt and return to the magma. | 1 |
| 4 (a) (i) | Lead(II) sulphide + oxygen → lead(II) oxide + sulphur dioxide<br>$2\,PbS\,(s) + 3O_2(g) \rightarrow 2\,PbO(s) + 2SO_2(g)$ | 2 |

Letts Q&A

| Question | Answer | Mark |
|---|---|---|

**Examiner's tip** For grade C or above, on either Foundation or Higher tier, you would be expected to write a balanced symbolic equation. Unless you are very confident, it is worth writing a word equation first, to help you. Then you have to write the correct formulae for lead(II) sulphide, oxygen, lead(II) oxide and sulphur dioxide. Remember, oxygen exists in molecules as pairs of atoms so you have to write $O_2$. Finally, you have to balance the equation. Notice in the unbalanced equation that you have three oxygen atoms on the right-hand side. This should suggest doubling the numbers of lead(II) oxide and sulphur dioxide on the right-hand side and using three molecules of oxygen. There are two marks for a correctly balanced equation and one mark if you make a slight slip, e.g. 6O instead of $3O_2$. The question does not ask you to include state symbols, so there is no mark for them (but include them if you can as they give a positive impression to the examiner).

(ii) Sulphur dioxide escaping into the atmosphere can form sulphurous and sulphuric acids. **1**
These acids can attack metals and rocks. They can also make lakes and rivers more acidic. **1**

(iii) Sulphur dioxide is a raw material in the manufacture of sulphuric acid. **1**

(b) (i) Reduction. **1**

(ii) You will need to get relative atomic masses from a Periodic Table.
Pb = 208 and O = 16.
From the equation,
448 tonnes of lead(II) oxide needs 12 tonnes of pure carbon. **1**
So, 10 tonnes of lead(II) oxide needs $12 \times {}^{10}/_{448}$ tonnes of pure carbon. **1**
= 0.27 tonnes **1**
However, carbon used is only 90% pure, so amount required is
$0.27 \times {}^{10}/_{9}$ tonnes **1**
= 0.30 tonnes. **1**

**Examiner's tip** This calculation is very involved and is worth a total of 5 marks. It is important to write down all the steps, to ensure you get full credit and also so marks can be given for correct working even if you get a wrong answer.

(c) (i) The silver will dissolve mostly in the zinc **True**.
A silver-lead mixture will form on top of the zinc **False**.
Lead will float on top of the silver-zinc liquid mixture. **False**.
A silver-zinc mixture will form on top of the molten lead **True**. **2**

(ii) Silver is a more expensive metal than tin or lead. **1**

**Examiner's tip** It is unlikely that you are familiar with this way of extracting silver. You are not meant to recall knowledge, but to use the information in the question.

(d) (i) Any three of the following:

Make hot solutions of lead(II) nitrate and sodium chloride.
Mix the hot solutions and allow them to cool slowly.
Crystals of lead(II) chloride form on cooling.
Filter off the crystals, wash and dry. **3**

Lead(II) nitrate + sodium chloride → lead(II) chloride + sodium chloride
$Pb(NO_3)_2(aq) + 2NaCl(aq) \rightarrow PbCl_2(s) + 2NaNO_3(aq)$ **1**

| Question | | Answer | Mark |
|---|---|---|---|
| | (ii) | When pieces of lead(II) oxide react with cold hydrochloric acid, a layer of insoluble lead(II) chloride is formed which prevents the lead(II) oxide and hydrochloric acid coming into contact. | 1 |

**Examiner's tip** This is an example of a preparation on an insoluble salt by precipitation. It is, however, a difficult example because of the solubility of lead(II) chloride in cold and hot water.

| | | | | |
|---|---|---|---|---|
| 5 | (a) | | Sulphur dioxide. | 1 |
| | (b) | (i) | Neutralisation. | 1 |
| | | (ii) | Water. | 1 |
| | (c) | | $Zn^{2+} + 2e^- \rightarrow Zn$ | 1 |
| | (d) | | Galvanising steel to prevent corrosion or making alloys, e.g. brass. | 1 |

**Examiner's tip** There are other possible uses for zinc, such as dry cell batteries.

## 4 AIR AND ATMOSPHERE

| Question | | Answer | Mark |
|---|---|---|---|
| 1 | (a) | Gas X – carbon dioxide; Gas Y – oxygen. | 1 |
| | (b) | Respiration and combustion of carbon compounds produce carbon dioxide. | 1 |
| | | Photosynthesis removes carbon dioxide and adds oxygen to keep the oxygen-carbon dioxide balance. | 1 |
| 2 | (a) | Carbon dioxide. | 1 |
| | (b) | Any one of the following:<br>Decay of organic waste in landfill sites/marshes/compost heaps/released by termites or cows. | 1 |
| | (c) | Sulphur dioxide from the factory reacts with water (and oxygen) in the air to make sulphurous and sulphuric acids. | 1 |
| | | Sulphurous acid and sulphuric acid attack the stonework. | 1 |

**Examiner's tip** A good answer here could include some equations.

$SO_2(g) + H_2O(l) \rightleftharpoons H_2SO_3(aq)$

$H_2SO_3(aq) + [O] \rightarrow H_2SO_4(aq)$

If the stonework was calcium carbonate:

$CaCO_3(s) + H_2SO_4(aq) \rightarrow CaSO_4(s) + H_2O(l) + CO_2(g)$

| | | | |
|---|---|---|---|
| | (d) | Immediately after 1956 levels of sulphur dioxide fell very little. | 1 |
| | | Immediately after 1968 the levels of sulphur dioxide dropped considerably. | 1 |

Letts Q&A

**Question** **Answer** **Mark**

***Examiner's tip*** It is easy to drop a mark here. You must make some sort of comparison between what happened after 1956 and after 1968. A one mark answer could be 'the level of sulphur dioxide dropped off after 1968'.

**3** (a) Propane. **1**

***Examiner's tip*** Remember we are dealing with negative numbers.

(b) (i)

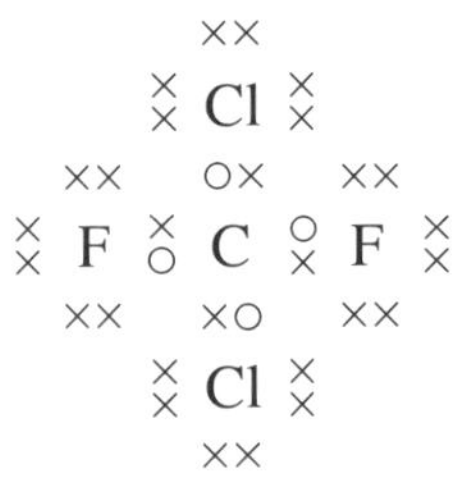

Correct arrangement of atoms. **1**
Correct arrangement of electrons. **1**

(ii) Covalent bonding. **1**

(iii) CFCs destroy the ozone layer.
CFCs break up to give chlorine atoms.
Chlorine atoms react and destroy ozone.
Ozone removes most dangerous UV radiation from Sun.
Holes in ozone layer over poles **3**

***Examiner's tip*** Any three points are given a mark each. In this kind of question candidates produce a wide range of answers. Any answer that is correct chemistry will receive credit, even if not given on the mark scheme.

(iv) Compound: Propane. **1**
Reasons: It has a boiling point very similar to that of CFC. It is the boiling point which is important in a change from liquid to gas. **1**

## 5 QUANTITATIVE CHEMISTRY

**Question** **Answer** **Mark**

**1** (a) $OH^- + H^+ \rightarrow H_2O$ **2**

***Examiner's tip*** Ionic equations cause students a lot of problems. The atoms on the left hand side and on the right hand side must be there in equal numbers just as in any equation. The charges must also balance. Here the charges on both sides add to zero.

(b) (i) 27.5°C **1**

| Question | | Answer | Mark |
|---|---|---|---|
| | (ii) | The equation shows 15 $cm^3$ of sodium hydroxide solution reacts with 35 $cm^3$ of hydrochloric acid. | 1 |
| | | Both solutions contain the same number of moles. | 1 |
| (c) | | Mass of 1 mole of NaOH = 40 g. | 1 |
| | | 100 g of sodium hydroxide contains 100/40 moles = 2.5 moles. | 1 |
| | | 2.5 mol/$dm^3$. | 1 |
| (d) | | Mass of 1 mole of sodium chloride = 58.5 g. | 1 |
| | | From the equation 40 g NaOH produces 58.5 g NaCl, | 1 |
| | | 100 g NaOH produces 146.3 g NaCl. | 1 |

**Examiner's tip** It is important here to go back to the equation at the start of the question. If an equation is given in a question you should expect to use it throughout the question.

| Question | | Answer | Mark |
|---|---|---|---|
| (e) | | Sodium conducts electricity because of the presence of free electrons. These move within the structure to carry the charge. | 1 |
| | | In molten sodium chloride ions are free to move and these carry the charge. | 1 |

**Examiner's tip** Appreciating the difference in the way electricity is carried through a metal and through a molten electrolyte is a good indicator of an A* candidate.

**2** (a)

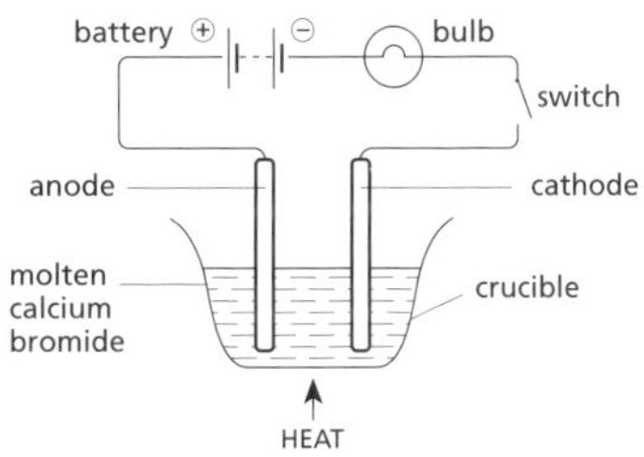


| Question | | Answer | Mark |
|---|---|---|---|
| | | A labelled circuit with switch, bulb, battery. | 1 |
| | | Anode and cathode correctly labelled. | 1 |
| | | Suitable heated container for calcium bromide. | 1 |
| (b) | (i) | Quantity of electricity passed = current × time | 1 |
| | | = 5 × 193 = 965 coulombs | 1 |
| | (ii) | Number of Faradays = 965/96500 = 0.01 Faradays | 1 |
| | (iii) | 2 Faradays of electricity produce 1 mole of calcium atoms. | 1 |
| | | 0.01 Faradays produce 0.005 moles of calcium atoms. | 1 |
| | (iv) | 1 Faraday of electricity produces 1 mole of bromine atoms. | 1 |
| | | 0.01 Faradays of electricity produce 0.01 moles of bromine atoms. | 1 |
| (c) | | The gap between the electrodes is filled with calcium which conducts electricity. | 1 |
| (d) | | Hydrogen gas. | 1 |

| Question | | Answer | Mark |
|---|---|---|---|
| | | Formed by reaction of calcium with water. | 1 |
| | | $Ca + 2H_2O \rightarrow Ca(OH)_2 + H_2$ | 1 |
| 3 | (a) | Pipette (measuring cylinder is not accurate enough). | 1 |
| | (b) | Indicator (methyl orange) changes colour. | 1 |
| | (c) | $Na_2CO_3(aq) + 2HCl(aq) \rightarrow 2NaCl(aq) + CO_2(g) + H_2O(l)$ | 2 |

**Examiner's tip** Phenolphthalein is another indicator but it changes colour at a higher pH when the following reaction takes place.

$$Na_2CO_3(aq) + HCl(aq) \rightarrow NaHCO_3(aq) + NaCl(aq)$$

The volume of acid required for this process is half the volume required when using methyl orange as indicator.

| Question | | Answer | Mark |
|---|---|---|---|
| | (d) | $20.0\,cm^3$ of 0.25 M hydrochloric acid. | |
| | | Number of moles in $1000\,cm^3$ of 0.25 M acid = 0.25 | |
| | | No. of moles in $20\,cm^3$ of 0.25 M acid = $0.25 \times 20/1000$ | 1 |
| | | = 0.005 moles | 1 |
| | (e) | 0.005 moles of acid reacts with $25\,cm^3$ of sodium carbonate | |
| | | $0.005 \times 1000/25$ moles of acid react with $1000\,cm^3$ sodium carbonate solution | 1 |
| | | = 0.2 moles | 1 |
| | (f) | From the equation, 2 moles of acid react with 1 mole of sodium carbonate. | 1 |
| | | No. of moles of sodium carbonate = 0.1 moles | 1 |
| | (g) | Mass of sodium carbonate = $0.1 \times M_r(Na_2CO_3)$ | 1 |
| | | = 10.6 g | 1 |
| | (h) | **10.6 g** of anhydrous sodium carbonate combines with **18 g** of water to produce 28.6 g of sodium carbonate crystals. | 1 |
| | (i) | 180 g | 1 |
| | (j) | 10 | 1 |

**Examiner's tip** This could be a difficult calculation, but splitting it into stages helps you to work through it.

| Question | | Answer | Mark |
|---|---|---|---|
| 4 | (a) | The solutes will dissolve faster in warm water. | 1 |
| | (b) | Sodium hydroxide solution is 80 g/l (or 80 g per $dm^3$) | |
| | | 1 mole of sodium hydroxide = (23 + 16 + 1) = 40 g | 1 |
| | | Concentration of sodium hydroxide = 80/40 = 2 mol/1 | 1 |
| | (c) | For cold brown colour: | |
| | | $10\,cm^3$ of sodium sulphide solution is added to $40\,cm^3$ of sodium hydroxide solution to make $50\,cm^3$ of toner. | |
| | | $20\,cm^3$ of sodium sulphide solution is added to $80\,cm^3$ of sodium | |

| Question | | | Answer | Mark |
|---|---|---|---|---|
| | | | hydroxide solution to make 100 $cm^3$ of toner. | 1 |
| | | | Solution contains 20 × 100/1000 = 2 g of sodium sulphide. | 1 |
| 5 | (a) | (i) | 1 No calcium carbonate remains in the solution. | 1 |
| | | | 2 No bubbles of carbon dioxide are being produced. | 1 |

**Examiner's tip** Excess dilute hydrochloric acid tells us that all of the calcium carbonate would be used up when the reaction stops.

| | | | | |
|---|---|---|---|---|
| | | (ii) | It is possible that some solid remains in the flask. These are impurities which do not react with acid. | 1 |
| | (b) | | $H^+ (aq) + OH^- (aq) \rightarrow H_2O(l)$ | 2 |

**Examiner's tip** There are two marks for the correct balanced equation including state symbols. One mark is awarded for a slight mistake. This ionic equation is very important.

| | | | | |
|---|---|---|---|---|
| | (c) | (i) | Mass of hydrochloric acid = 20.00 − 2.48 = 17.52 g | 1 |
| | | (ii) | Mass of 1 mole of $CaCO_3$ = 40 + 12 + (3x16) = 100 g | 1 |
| | | | From the equation | |
| | | | 73 g of hydrochloric acid react with 100 g of calcium carbonate | 1 |
| | | | 17.52 g of hydrochloric acid reacts with $100 \times \frac{17.52}{73}$ g $CaCO_3$ | 1 |
| | | | = 24.0g | 1 |
| | | (iii) | Percentage purity of calcium carbonate = $100 \times \frac{24.0}{25.0}$ = 96% | 1 |

**Examiner's tip** It is worthwhile looking at your answer and checking it is reasonable.

## 6 THE PERIODIC TABLE

| Question | | Answer | Mark |
|---|---|---|---|
| 1 | (a) | 0.46 g of sodium combines with (0.62 − 0.46) g oxygen = 0.16 g. | 1 |
| | | Number of moles of sodium = 0.46/23 = 0.02 moles. | 1 |
| | | Number of moles of oxygen = 0.23/23 = 0.01 moles. | 1 |
| | | Empirical formula = $Na_2O$. | 1 |

**Examiner's tip** You must show all your working so the examiner can give you some reward if you make a mistake. The common mistake here is to write NaO2 for the empirical formula not Na2O.
There are twice as many atoms of sodium as oxygen.

(b) (i)

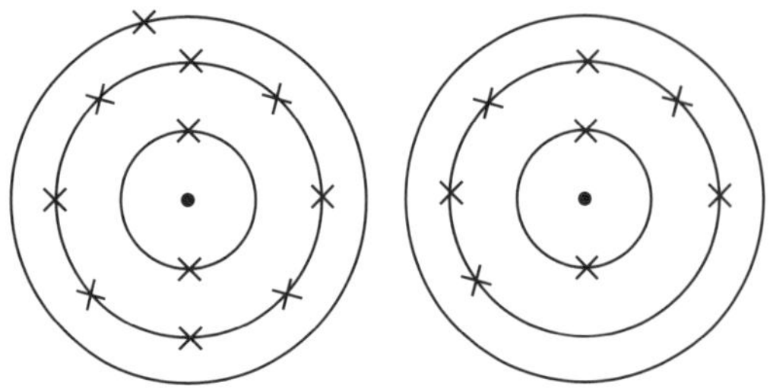


2

**Examiner's tip** Here you must show the complete electronic structure with inner electrons.

(ii) Sodium atom loses one electron 1
and forms a sodium ion, $Na^+$ ion. 1
Oxygen atom gains two electrons 1
and forms an oxide ion, $O^{2-}$. 1

**Examiner's tip** Ionic bonding involves a complete transfer of electrons to form ions. The ions are charged and held together by electrostatic forces.

(c) Two points from:
Sodium floats on the water, as a molten ball, moves over the surface, fizzes and gives off a gas. 2

**Examiner's tip** Notice the emphasis in the question on what you would see. This is common. It is a demonstration experiment you should remember. If you wrote hydrogen produced, or sodium hydroxide produced, or the water gets hot these could not receive credit.

(d) (i) 2,8,8 1

(ii) Atoms do not bond together, so monatomic. 1
This is an arrangement where loss or gain of electrons does not take place. 1

**2** (a) **A** 1

(b) **E** 1

(c) **C** and **D**. 1

**Examiner's tip** E and F are gases. However, F is in Group 0 and elements in Group 0 are composed of single atoms rather than pairs of atoms. If you are confused about groups and periods, you could give B and F incorrectly for (c).

**3** (a) Barium, strontium, calcium, magnesium. 1

| Question | Answer | Mark |
|---|---|---|

**Examiner's tip** For some syllabuses you are expected to know some chemistry of Group II (alkaline Earth metals). Other syllabuses do not require you to study this group particularly, but you would be expected to answer this question using your knowledge of trends within the Periodic Table. Make sure you put them in order of decreasing reactivity as stated. Many students get the right sequence, but put them in order of increasing reactivity. No marks for that!

| Question | Answer | Mark |
|---|---|---|
| (b) | Reacts very slowly with cold water. | **1** |

**Examiner's tip** You should use the pattern of reactivity in the Periodic Table to predict this reaction. Any answer which implies less reaction than magnesium would be acceptable – even no reaction.

| Question | Answer | Mark |
|---|---|---|
| (c) | Under petroleum oil. | **1** |

**Examiner's tip** You should appreciate the reactivity of barium is similar to that of alkali metals. It could perhaps be stored in a similar way.

| Question | Answer | Mark |
|---|---|---|
| (d) (i) | Name Barium chloride | **1** |
| | Formula $BaCl_2$ | **1** |
| (ii) | Ionic bonding. | **1** |
| | $Ba^{2+}$ and $Cl^-$ | **1** |
| | Barium, two $e^-$ in outer energy level are lost to form ion; Cl gains one $e^-$ to form $Cl^-$ | **1** |

## 7 RATES OF REACTION

| Question | Answer | Mark |
|---|---|---|
| **1** (a) | **D** | **1** |

**Examiner's tip** There are different ways of coming up with the correct answer here. One way is to notice that C, D and F take place at 40°C and the others at 20°C. In C and D a powder is used and so reactions will be faster. In D the acid is 4 mol/l rather than 1 mol/l.

| Question | Answer | Mark |
|---|---|---|
| (b) | **A** and **E**. | **1** |

**Examiner's tip** You should be looking for two reactions where all the conditions are the same except one uses lumps and one uses powder. In some other possible pairs, e.g. B and D or E and F, one reaction is at 20° C and the other 40° C.

| Question | | | Answer | Mark |
|---|---|---|---|---|
| 2 | (a) | (i) | Choice of suitable scales for x and y axis. | 1 |
| | | | Plotting. | 1 |
| | | | Curve not going through an anomalous result. | 1 |

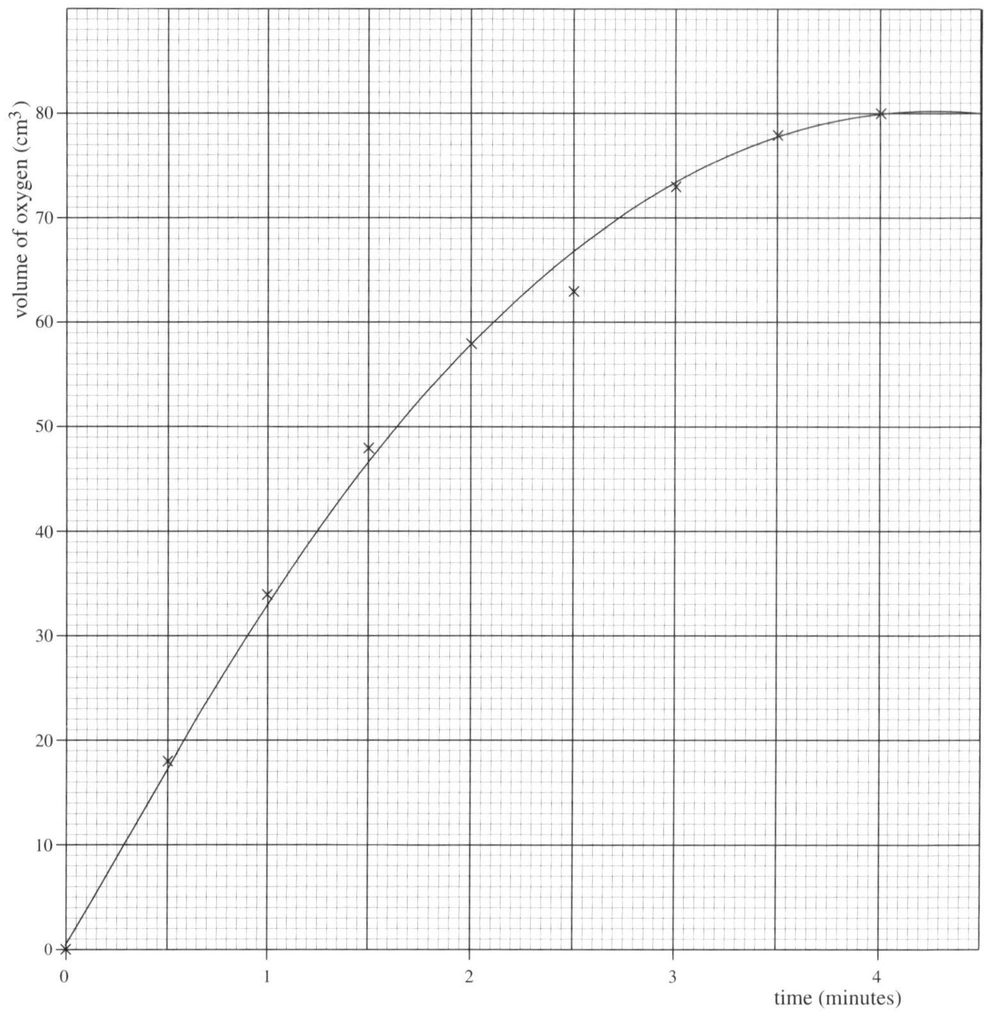


**Examiner's tip** This is a typical graph for candidates working at A*–B (high demand). It requires getting the scales right so the graph fills the whole paper, plotting, recognising that the result at 2.5 minutes is an anomalous result and drawing a curve ignoring it. Three marks hard earned.

| Question | | | Answer | Mark |
|---|---|---|---|---|
| | | (ii) | At the start of the experiment there are more hydrogen peroxide particles in the solution. | 1 |
| | | | Results in more effective collisions leading to reaction. | 1 |
| | (b) | | The curve drawn should be steeper than the one plotted (because there is a larger surface of catalyst for reaction). | 1 |
| | | | The curve should reach the same maximum (before 4 minutes) as the same quantity of hydrogen peroxide is present. | 1 |

| Question | Answer | Mark |
|---|---|---|

**Examiner's tip** You can only provide a sketch.

## 8 INDUSTRIAL PROCESSES

| Question | | | Answer | Mark |
|---|---|---|---|---|
| 1 | (a) | (i) | Process A Fractional distillation (of air). | 1 |
| | | (ii) | Process B Haber process (or synthesis). | 1 |
| | | (iii) | Process D Neutralisation. | 1 |
| | (b) | | Fertiliser. | 1 |
| | (c) | | Temperature about 450° C. | 1 |
| | | | High pressure (up to 1000 atm). | 1 |
| | | | Catalyst – finely divided iron. | 1 |

**Examiner's tip** It is important that you know the conditions for the Haber process.

| Question | | | Answer | Mark |
|---|---|---|---|---|
| | (d) | (i) | Exothermic reaction. | 1 |
| | | (ii) | 17 tonnes produces 1 + 14 + (3 × 16) tonnes of nitric acid | 1 |
| | | | = 63 tonnes | 1 |

**Examiner's tip** Examiners are required to set questions testing social, economic, technological and environmental aspects of chemistry. Questions on industrial processes provide good opportunities.

| Question | | | Answer | Mark |
|---|---|---|---|---|
| 2 | (a) | (i) | Calcium carbonate. | 1 |
| | | (ii) | Advantages – provide raw materials for industry, provide jobs for workers, provide new roads, etc., bring money into local economy, etc. Any two. | 2 |
| | | | Disadvantages – noise, unsightly quarries, increased traffic on roads, dust, etc. Any two | 2 |

**Examiner's tip** It is not always clear when marking which the candidate thinks is an advantage and which a disadvantage. Make clear whether you are writing about advantages or disadvantages. Here you must give two of each.

| Question | | | Answer | Mark |
|---|---|---|---|---|
| | (b) | | Property of aluminium – good conductor of heat, malleable. | 1 |
| | | | Use of copper – water pipes. | 1 |
| | | | Lead. | 1 |

**Examiner's tip** Your answer must fit. For example copper for electrical wiring would not be correct.

| Question | | Answer | Mark |
|---|---|---|---|
| (c) | (i) | $Fe_3O_4 + 4CO \rightarrow 3Fe + 4CO_2$ | 1 |
| | (ii) | Carbon monoxide is oxidised | 1 |

**Examiner's tip** Carbon monoxide is oxidised because oxygen is added.

| | | | |
|---|---|---|---|
| | (iii) | Calcium carbonate (or limestone) | 1 |
| (d) | (i) | ${}^{14}_{6}C \rightarrow {}^{14}_{7}N + {}^{0}_{-1}e$ | |
| | | One mark for each product. | 2 |
| | (ii) | Two half lives (100 to 50 and 50 to 25), | 1 |
| | | 11460 years. | 1 |

**Examiner's tip** Part (d) will probably be found on Physics papers in most syllabuses.

# 9 WATER

| Question | | | Answer | Mark |
|---|---|---|---|---|
| 1 | (a) | (i) | Any two of: effervescence/fizzing/bubbling; solid dissolves/disappears; forms colourless solution. | 2 |

**Examiner's tip** It is important that you include only observations.

| | | | | |
|---|---|---|---|---|
| | | (ii) | $BaCO_3 + 2HCl \rightarrow BaCl_2 + CO_2 + H_2O$ | 2 |

**Examiner's tip** One mark is for correct formulae and one for balancing.

| | | | | |
|---|---|---|---|---|
| | | (iii) | $Ba^{2+} + SO_4^{2-} \rightarrow BaSO_4$ | 2 |

**Examiner's tip** Two marks for correct equation. Allow one mark for one error.

| | | | | |
|---|---|---|---|---|
| | (b) | | Three points to be included in the answer for one mark each. Dissolve barium chloride in water, add acid and filter off precipitate, wash and dry. | 3 |
| | (c) | (i) | Barium sulphate is insoluble/very sparingly soluble/does not enter body or blood. | 1 |
| | | (ii) | Either: forms barium chloride which is soluble/poisonous; or, would form soluble/poisonous barium salt. | 1 |

**Examiner's tip** It is not sufficient to write that barium carbonate reacts with hydrochloric acid.

| Question | Answer | Mark |
|---|---|---|
| 2 (a) (i) | $KNO_3$ | |
| | Mass of 1 mole of potassium nitrate = 39 + 14 + (3 × 16) = 101 g | 1 |
| | Percentage of nitrogen = $\frac{14 \times 100}{101}$ = 13.9% | 1 |
| (ii) | $(NH_4)_2SO_4$ | |
| | Mass of 1 mole = 2(14 + 4) + 32 + (4 × 16) = 132 g | 1 |
| | Percentage of nitrogen = $\frac{28 \times 100}{132}$ = 21.2% | 1 |

**Examiner's tip** Don't forget there are two moles of nitrogen atoms in each mole of ammonium sulphate.

| Question | Answer | Mark |
|---|---|---|
| (b) | 1 Potassium nitrate contains another element (potassium) essential for plant growth. | |
| | 2 Potassium nitrate is less soluble than ammonium sulphate. | |
| | 3 Nitrates absorbed by plants better than ions. (any two) | 2 |

**Examiner's tip** As a general rule, ammonium compounds are very soluble in water. At 20° C the solubilities of ammonium sulphate and potassium nitrate are 70 g/100 g of water and 14 g/100 g of water respectively.

| Question | Answer | Mark |
|---|---|---|
| (c) | Any three of the following: | |
| | Excess fertiliser is washed off fields into rivers. | |
| | Bacteria in river oxidise ammonia to nitrates. | |
| | Reduces dissolved oxygen concentration in water. | |
| | Nitrogen encourages plant growth. | |
| | This prevents light entering/reduces photosynthesis. | |
| | Decaying plants use up oxygen. | |
| | Fish die. | 3 |
| 3 (a) | 81 g | 1 |
| (b) | 33 g | 1 |
| (c) | 48 g | 1 |
| (d) | Filter off the potassium dichromate crystals. | 1 |
| | Wash with a small volume of water and dry. | 1 |

**Examiner's tip** Quantitative interpretation of solubility curves is an important aspect of Higher tier papers.

| Question | Answer | Mark |
|---|---|---|
| 4 (a) (i) | Calcium hydrogencarbonate. | 1 |

**Examiner's tip** You should know that calcium hydrogencarbonate causes temporary hardness in water. However, the high concentration of calcium and hydrogen-carbonate ions in the sample is a good clue.

| Question | Answer | Mark |
|---|---|---|
| (ii) | Method Addition of sodium carbonate crystals. | 1 |
| | Explanation Sodium carboante precipitates calcium sulphate and removes calcium ions in solution. | 1 |

| Question | Answer | Mark |
|---|---|---|
| | $CaSO_4(aq) + Na_2CO_3(aq) \rightarrow CaSO_4(s) + Na_2SO_4(aq)$<br>or $Ca^{2+}(aq) + SO_4^{2-}(aq) \rightarrow CaSO_4(s)$ | 1 |

**Examiner's tip** Note the question is now about permanent hardness. Some candidates will not read this and give a good answer for temporary hardness and receive no marks.

| Question | Answer | Mark |
|---|---|---|
| (b) | Calcium carbonate. | 1 |
| (c) | When soap is added to hard water, a precipitate of calcium stearate is formed. This uses up the soap and reduces lather.<br>$2C_{17}H_{35}COO^{-}Na^{+} + Ca^{2+}(aq) \rightarrow (C_{17}H_{35}COO^{-})_2Ca^{2+} + 2Na^{2+}$<br>Calcium stearate is scum. | 3 |

# 10 MOCK EXAMINATION PAPER

| Question | Answer | Mark |
|---|---|---|
| 1 (a) (i) | Hydrogen nucleus, chlorine nucleus, electron from hydrogen, electron from chlorine. | 4 |
| (ii) | Covalent bonding. | 1 |
| (b) (i) | 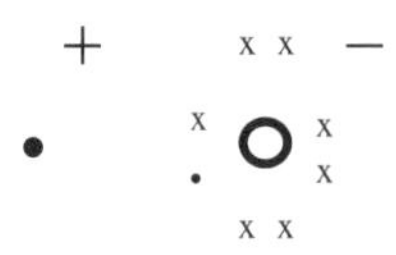 (One mark for each ion.) | 2 |
| (ii) | Test electrical conductivity of solution, | 1 |
| | solution containing ions conducts electricity. | 1 |
| (iii) | Named suitable indicator, e.g. litmus. Indicator turns to acid colour – red in the case of litmus. | 2 |
| (c) (i) | Test with limewater. Limewater turns milky. | 2 |
| (ii) | $2H^{+} + CO_3^{2-} \rightarrow CO_2 + H_2O$ | 2 |

**Examiner's tip** Candidates frequently confuse ionic and covalent bonding. Remember ionic bonding involves a complete transfer of electrons and ionic bonding only a sharing of electrons. Don't forget to give the result of the tests.

| Question | Answer | Mark |
|---|---|---|
| 2 (a) | Water containing dissolved calcium and **magnesium** compounds is said to be hard water. Hard water does not lather well with **soap**, but forms **scum**. | 3 |
| (b) (i) | Measuring cylinder/pipette. | 1 |
| (ii) | Burette. | 1 |
| (iii) | Q | 1 |
| (c) | P contains only permanent hardness.<br>The volume of soap is the same before and after boiling,<br>Q contains both permanent and temporary hardness.<br>The volume of soap solution is reduced after boiling, but not down to $0.5\,cm^3$.<br>R contains temporary hardness only. | |

| Question | | | Answer | Mark |
|---|---|---|---|---|
| | | | The volume of soap is reduced to 0.5 $cm^3$ after boiling. | **6** |
| | (d) | | Temporary hardness is caused by dissolved **calcium hydrogencarbonate**. This is formed when rocks containing **calcium carbonate** are dissolved by rainwater. Permanent hardness is caused by dissolved **calcium sulphate**. Hard water can be softened by using **sodium carbonate**. | **4** |

***Examiner's tip*** This question requires you to use the data given. Remember that temporary hardness is removed by boiling and permanent hardness is not.

| Question | | | Answer | Mark |
|---|---|---|---|---|
| **3** | (a) | (i) | 1.12 g | **1** |
| | | (ii) | 0.02 | **1** |
| | | (iii) | 2.13g | **1** |
| | | (iv) | 0.06 | **1** |
| | | (v) | $FeCl_3$ | **1** |
| | (b) | (i) | 5.6 g of iron combines with 7.1 g of chlorine.<br>5.6/56 moles of iron combine with 7.1/35.5 moles of chlorine.<br>0.1 moles of iron combine with 0.2 moles of chlorine. | **3** |
| | | (ii) | $Fe(s) + 2HCl(g) \rightarrow FeCl_2(s) + H_2(g)$<br>(One mark for correct formulae, one mark for balancing, one mark for state symbols.) | **3** |
| | (c) | | When sodium hydroxide is added to iron(II) chloride, iron(II) hydroxide is precipitated. $FeCl_2 + 2NaOH \rightarrow Fe(OH)_2 + 2NaCl$<br>Iron(II) hydroxide is green. This is oxidised by oxygen in the air.<br>$4Fe(OH)_2 + O_2 + 2H_2O \rightarrow 4Fe(OH)_3$ | **5** |
| | (d) | | Any three of the following:<br>high density, shiny/strong magnetic properties/good catalyst (Haber process) forms more than one ion/coloured compounds. | **3** |

***Examiner's tip*** This is a difficult question, especially part (c) which certainly has marks targeted at A*. Calculating a formula from reacting masses, writing balanced symbol equations are important.

| Question | | | Answer | Mark |
|---|---|---|---|---|
| **4** | (a) | (i) | An addition reaction is where two molecules react to form a single product. | **1** |
| | | (ii) | $C_2H_4 + H_2O \rightarrow C_2H_5OH$ | **1** |
| | (b) | (i) | Any eight of the following:<br>Reaction takes place in the presence of an enzyme.<br>Correctly named enzyme – zymase.<br>In the absence of air or oxygen.<br>Other product is carbon dioxide.<br>Temperature kept between 30–40° C.<br>Process is called fermentation.<br>Stops when about 13% ethanol present.<br>Reaction slightly exothermic.<br>Prevent outside enzymes from entering.<br>$C_6H_{12}O_6(aq) \rightarrow 2C_2H_5OH\ (aq) + 2CO_2(g)$ | **8** |
| | | (ii) | Fractional distillation. | **2** |

| Question | Answer | Mark |
|---|---|---|
| | Ethanol and water have different boiling points. | 1 |
| (c) | Great Britain has deposits of oil, which are a source of ethene. | 1 |
| | In Brazil, with plenty of sunlight, sugars are easily produced by photosynthesis. | 1 |

**Examiner's tip** Part (b)(i) is an example of extended writing. There are eight marks available. You must make at least eight points. Make sure you include conditions and the equation.

| Question | Answer | Mark |
|---|---|---|
| 5 (a) (i) | **B** | 1 |
| (ii) | **B** and **C**. | 2 |
| (iii) | **A** | 1 |
| (b) (i) | Heat each substance. Substance with a giant structure will have a high melting point. Substance with a molecular structure will have a low melting point. | 3 |
| (ii) | Test the electrical conductivity of the substance when it is molten. A substance with a giant structure of ions will conduct electricity when molten. A substance with a giant structure of atoms will not. | 3 |

**Examiner's tip** It is important in (b)(ii) to test the electrical conductivity when the substances are molten. An ionic solid, such as sodium chloride, does not conduct electricity when solid because the ions are not free to move.

**Marking your test**

Use the marking scheme to mark your test. If you are not sure about any of your answers, ask your teacher. When you have a mark for the test out of 75 marks, you can use this table to estimate your likely grade. Remember, however, that this is just one test and so you cannot be sure you will get this grade every time. It will give you an indication of your level of achievement.

| Mark in the test | Grade |
|---|---|
| Over 68 | A* |
| 60–67 | A |
| 49–59 | B |
| 38–48 | C |
| 18–37 | D |
| Less than 18 | Ungraded |